HANDBOOK IN DIAGNOSTIC TEACHING:

A LEARNING DISABILITIES APPROACH

ABRIDGED EDITION

Philip H. Mann
Research Associate
Applied Social Science
University of Miami
Coral Gables, Florida

Patricia Suiter
Director, House of Learning
Miami, Florida

ALLYN AND BACON, INC.
Boston • London • Sydney • Toronto

Abridged edition of HANDBOOK IN DIAGNOSTIC TEACHING: A LEARNING DISABILITIES APPROACH, © Copyright 1974 by Allyn and Bacon, Inc., 470 Atlantic Avenue, Boston.

All rights reserved. No part of the material protected by this copyright notice may be reproduced or utilized in any form or by any means, electronic or mechanical, including photocopying, recording, or by any informational storage and retrieval system without written permission from the copyright owner.

Library of Congress Catalog Card Number: 73-89164
Printed in the United States of America

ISBN: 0-205-04416-6
Ninth printing . . . April, 1978

CONTENTS

Foreword v
Preface vii

CHAPTER 1 • THEORETICAL PERSPECTIVES   1

    Why Children Fail   3
    Explanation of Design of Learning Correlates   6
        Verbal Learning Systems   8
        Non-Verbal Learning Systems   13

CHAPTER 2 • DEVELOPMENTAL SPELLING INVENTORIES   17

    Developing A Spelling Inventory   17
    Screening Procedures   18
    Spelling Errors to Look For   18
    Mann-Suiter Developmental Spelling Inventory   19

CHAPTER 3 • DEVELOPMENTAL READING INVENTORIES   21

    Developing Your Own Word Reading Inventory   21
    Administration of Developmental Word Recognition
      Inventory   30
    Scoring of Developmental Word Reading Inventories   31
    Word Reading Errors to Look For   31
    Checking for Oral Language Development   32
    Developing Your Own Developmental Paragraph
      Reading Inventory   34
    Screening Procedures for the Developmental
      Paragraph Reading Inventory   36
    Scoring Procedures for the Developmental
      Paragraph Reading Inventory   37
    Scoring of Comprehension Questions   38
    Finding the Reading Levels   38
    Silent Reading Comprehension   39
    Listening Comprehension Level   39

Contents

        Reading Errors to Look For   40
        Mann-Suiter Developmental Reading Summary Record   41
        Mann-Suiter Developmental Paragraph Reading
          Inventory   42

CHAPTER 4 • SUPPLEMENTARY EVALUATION AND SPECIAL FORMS   53

        General Readiness   53
        Auditory   54
        Visual   55
        Visual Motor   55
        Language   56
        Social Emotional   56
        Mann-Suiter Analysis of Errors Sheets   56
        Mann-Suiter Diagnostic Worksheet   61
        Mann-Suiter Educational Profile   65

CHAPTER 5 • DEFICIT LEVEL CURRICULUM (PROCESS ORIENTED)   67

        Auditory Channel   68
        Visual Channel   72
        Motor   78
        Language   87
        Control Factors   99
        Motivational And Emotional Factors   101

CHAPTER 6 • TASK LEVEL CURRICULUM   107

        Reading   107
          Initial and Remedial Teaching Approaches   107
          Modified Experience Approach to Reading   119
          Mann-Suiter Developmental Phrases   120
          Mann-Suiter Everyday Word List   127
        Spelling   126
        Handwriting   133
          Handwriting Screen   137
        Language   139
        Arithmetic   141

GLOSSARY   153
BIBLIOGRAPHY   161

FOREWORD

Since the advent of the educational measurements movement about a half century ago, teachers have been given advice by testers and diagnosticians of many kinds. Unfortunately, the teachers more often have been intimidated by the psychometrics than helped by the results. Much of the testing has been too peripheral to the instructional situation or too general to be useful. On the basis of test results teachers have often been advised, for example, that a child may be "expected" to achieve well or that he is "reading below capacity." At best such information is fraught with error, but the more fundamental difficulty is that it fails even to approach the kind of specificity required to organize instruction. The teacher's work is to influence the development of children through detailed and continuing instruction and it is in the interior of that process that help is needed.

Lately, teachers have pressed their claim for more helpful consultation and technical assistance at the level of specific instructional decisions for individual children. Some genuinely helpful and promising developments have emerged, such as the work on criterion-referenced testing, program evaluation, task analysis, and "precision teaching." In a broader context, new systems for managing assessments and instruction in classroom settings are being developed, for example, the Individually Guided Education (IGE) program advanced by the University of Wisconsin R & D Center. Hopefully, we are at the dawn of a new day in which the technicians and theorists will address the critical and detailed aspects of instruction to meet the individual needs of children.

Another main thrust in education is in the ways schools treat children who present exceptional needs of various kinds. Currently, the trend is to provide for such children by enhancing their regular classroom situations whenever possible, rather than by resorting to displacement of them to special classes or centers. This effort—"mainstreaming"—permits the bypassing of many of the stigmatizing labeling and segregating processes of more traditional approaches. However, "mainstreaming" also requires that regular classroom teachers know more about instruction of children with different learning patterns.

The Mann-Suiter book makes the contribution of adapting instruction to individual learning differences. The authors present a broad set of detailed and practical procedures by which the learning needs of individual children can be assessed and instruction in basic skills adapted. Diagnosis and teaching are made integral in a way that teachers can understand and will appreciate. Although the book assembles many ideas which are already on the educational scene, Mann and Suiter have creatively enlarged, synthesized, and organized them in a valuable format.

Foreword

The authors know very well that "mainstreaming" requires strong efforts to enhance the functioning of regular school programs. With their Miami colleagues they have been strong figures in pioneering methods by which regular classroom teachers and those who work with them are enabled to serve exceptional children in acquiring the basic tools of our culture within the mainstream of the community.

The ideas and techniques presented in this volume were developed and tested in practical teaching situations which involved both children and teachers. Heretofore, the ideas have been available only at conferences or through film; now the authors have made them available in an expanded form to a wider audience.

Mann and Suiter present no grand theory on the learning problems of children, nor do they claim to present a final word on any topic. Indeed, the publication format—in looseleaf binding—suggests their openness to additions and refinement. The reader who reviews this book systematically will find herein a marvelously useful set of tools in finished form and others in suggestions which teachers can adapt to create their own improvements in instruction.

Maynard C. Reynolds
Professor, Special Education
University of Minnesota

PREFACE

There is a trend today in the direction of modernizing and accelerating teacher training programs at different levels to include in-service as well as pre-service so that these individuals will be better able to function in schools that must accommodate to a changing society. Any new knowledge that is communicated to teachers through various training programs must reflect the combined pooling of information from individuals in various disciplines to include psychology, medicine, and social work, as well as the various areas within the arena of education itself. The interface between special education and regular classroom teachers, for example, must involve the acquisition of a common core of competencies and opportunities for working in concert with each other to achieve the best and most appropriate educational climate for children. There must also be a sharing of responsibility for the learning handicapped students who are failing in our public schools.

By delineating the critical skills necessary for success in the academic areas of reading, writing, spelling and arithmetic, teachers trained in the diagnostic teaching approach with aid from other professionals within the school will be better able to identify children's deficits in the language areas that prevent them from being successful in the given tasks.

Basic to this new era of accountability is the notion that teacher training institutions will become accountable not only to teachers but to the changing needs of the communities that they serve. Therefore, future looking programs must build into teachers at different levels the skills necessary to undertake a needs assessment and to select and apply methodology necessary to develop and evaluate sequential educational curriculum.

Evidence from many sources suggests that many educators lack the insights, skills, or incentives necessary to work with children who manifest a variety of learning difficulties. Teacher training programs at the pre-service level in most situations have not included course work and experiences that will enable their graduates to develop viable teaching strategies for learners who cannot profit from traditional educational techniques. Many children are being labeled lazy, emotionally disturbed, stupid, or mentally retarded. The teachers who are trying to educate these students are looking for materials that will do the job instead of looking at the children for clues as to how they may best learn. It can be said that they are "material centered" rather than "child centered" in their approach to teaching. This handbook was developed to fill the gap between what a teacher may already know about teaching children and what he needs to know in terms of teaching those who have difficulty in learning. It is also designed to create both an awareness of and a desire for additional knowledge

Preface

that will lead to the improvement of present day educational programs for learning handicapped children.

We would like to express our appreciation to Rose Marie McClung for her assistance with the manuscript, and to Ruth, for her encouragement and released time.

Dr. Philip H. Mann

CHAPTER 1

THEORETICAL PERSPECTIVES

There are many things about learning that educators have felt more or less intuitively for years, especially if they have had several years of experience with teaching children. Teachers have made reference to the "learning style" of a particular student. A great deal has been written about the "life styles" of individuals which to a large degree are formed by habit, economics and life experiences that are either positive or negative.

DIFFERENTIAL LEARNERS

More recently it has become evident that "learning style" and "life style" are more interrelated than had heretofore been commonly believed. Such an example would be the individual who is easily distracted in a school or classroom considered to be a high visual stimulus environment. He may also be the one who wears conservative, not too colorful clothes, and whose house or room is relatively free from excessive visual stimulation such as busy wallpaper, pictures, etc. A person who likes to study alone and is distracted by noise in the classroom, for example, may also desire a "quiet" place in his home, or he may avoid situations that "overload" him auditorially. Some teachers and children find it difficult to work in large "pods" or "open classrooms" and become easily fatigued or anxious by the end of the day. They expend more than the usual amount of energy in attempting to attend to many different tasks with excessive auditory and/or visual stimulation present.

There are a number of learners who have difficulty in processing information that is presented to them auditorially or visually. Some cannot learn efficiently when their auditory, visual, and tactual-kinesthetic processes are not synchronized to operate as a functional unit when attempting to learn or perform a particular task. By the same token, learning occurs in many children who have moderate deficiencies in certain processes that involve perception, imagery, language, and motor abilities while others who are only mildly involved fail at the same tasks. One explanation could be that the former compensates more effectively for the disability.

CHAP. 1   **Theoretical Perspectives**

Compensatory Processing

It appears that some individuals may be deficient in a particular learning process, *auditory-sequential memory* for example, which is necessary for the successful performance of a specific task. They will often compensate for this lack by utilizing to a greater degree related abilities or processes to complete the task. In cases of auditory sequential memory problems the students may use more visual associations to help them to remember rather than relying completely on auditory memory. A good example would be always writing down a phone number instead of depending solely on auditory memory. There are certain conditions, however, that must be met:

1. The processes utilized to compensate must be intact so that if the student is using visual clues or processes to compensate for a poor auditory memory, for example, these visual skills must be operating efficiently for him.
2. The learner must be motivated enough to want to compensate for his disability. Where there is no will to learn, there will be little learning.
3. The school must provide the learner with opportunities to use his intact learning skills. In teaching, for example, the instructor should furnish the student with associative aids such as a visual representation, i.e., concrete object or picture along with the symbol whenever possible so that the learner can associate the word with its visual referent. It appears that the basic principles of learning that are inherent in the associative learning theories apply here to a large degree. Individuals with learning disabilities quite often have difficulty "learning through discovery" expecially if they have problems in the areas of perception, imagery, or language. Associative clues, therefore, should be included whenever possible to reinforce learning. This means that objects, pictures, movement (tactual-kinesthetic), and real experiences to include opportunities to use manipulative materials such as clay, anagrams, etc., must be integrated as reinforcers into each of the skill or task level areas to be learned.

Programmatic Attack

Relying upon intact processing abilities, for example, depending mainly upon visual clues for learning to the extent that deficient auditory learning processes receive inferior attention, may result in a minimal utilization of these same auditory learning processes for new skill acquisition. For example, an individual who depends chiefly upon visual input because his auditory processing abilities are deficient may never really develop good auditory skills. He may, in fact, never trust his listening abilities. Opportunities for developing such deficient skills must be provided. This process is called *amelioration of the disabilities*. However, if one concentrates upon eliminating the deficit areas alone, the student may have little opportunity to achieve the task level function of reading, writing, or arithmetic. Thus, he may take years to become "ready" to learn. There is little evidence to support the contention that amelioration of the deficits alone will result in a better reader.

It is recommended that both the student's strengths and weaknesses be considered in setting up an instructional program. The teacher must be responsive to the needs of each student. The term "open channel" is familiarly associated with Anne Sullivan who discovered that Helen Keller could learn through her hand. The teacher must "decode" the student to discover the open channels, and, on the other hand, closed channels must be opened whenever possible for more integrated learning. The teacher must work concomitantly with the strengths at the task level as well as with the deficits in the daily educational program.

It is not illogical to conclude that reliance primarily upon intact learning abilities or correlates to the extent that deficient learning processes receive minimal utilization during the formative years results in an adult life style that stabilizes a particular pattern of learning reflecting this early disuse. As educators, we each must recognize that individuals learn differently and try to decode our own learning styles or patterns. We need to better understand ourselves and, even more importantly, try not to impose our "learning styles" on others. A teacher recently told of an experience where as a strong visual learner she required her students to "look up" and "focus in" before she presented a lesson. Her feeling was that "If they are not looking at me, they are not learning." However, problems began to arise when she received a 6'4" student teacher who was a strong auditory learner. He insisted that the students "tune in" and "listen up." Sometimes students listen better when they are not looking at you and vice versa. The important thing to consider is "Are they learning?"

There is presently a deep concern over how to teach language (reading, writing, spelling, arithmetic) to children who appear to have near average, average, or above average intelligence, but who have difficulty in learning. Although the basic integrity of their sensory input systems, such as auditory and visual acuity, is within normal range and speech and motor performance appear to be functioning adequately, learning does not take place at a normal pace. Thus, many learners have been described as exhibiting a "maturational lag." These students have been labeled as being neurologically impaired, perceptually handicapped, educationally handicapped, dyslexic, or as having specific learning disabilities.

The most obvious symptom, common to all these children, is the discrepancy in their learning between expected and actual achievement. They have been referred to as exhibiting a pattern of "hills and valleys" in their development, very high in some areas and very low in others. Many educators are recognizing the fact that there is too much variability in their development to simply label them as retarded or slow learners. These students display one or more significant deficits in essential learning processes and require specific educational techniques for initial as well as for remedial instruction.

In evaluating learning disabilities, the teacher needs to look at the child's level of development with regard to where he breaks down in the learning process, or more specifically to determine the problem areas that prevent him from learning a given task. Although for his age, a child may seem to have normal achievement possibilities and the potential to learn in some areas, in other areas he may be weak; and he will need special instruction or remediation which takes into account his specific problems. To be successful, the initial teaching and amelioration programs must be designed to consider both the student's strengths and weaknesses.

In order to do a more effective job of program planning or diagnostic teaching, the teacher needs to understand the components of each child's behavior patterns and the appropriate academic achievement levels for learners of different ages. He also must be prepared to utilize contributions from related disciplines such as medicine and psychology.

WHY CHILDREN FAIL

Educators must be continually aware of the fact that each learner is an individual, uniquely different in physical characteristics, personality, and general capacity but capable of learning

CHAP. 1 Theoretical Perspectives

and of making a contribution. They must also always consider physiological and social-emotional likenesses so that concern for differences is kept in the proper perspective.

Every child makes an accommodation to learning. Good or bad, this effort in many cases is the best that he can do. Unfortunately, the children who fail have not made a good accommodation to learning, especially in the area of communication skills.

It has become apparent to many educators that sometimes they wait too long for "readiness" to occur. It is questionable whether overall readiness is necessary for a child to learn a specific task. It is also obvious that some students need help to become "ready." Some teachers are attempting to facilitate readiness by providing children with activities that will better prepare them to become efficient learners. Since failure rather than success in school becomes the mode for so many students, it is necessary that we intervene as early as possible. This does not mean imposing inappropriate activities, but rather, that teachers cannot wait for an overall state of readiness in every area before starting to teach a child. Care must be taken, on the other hand, not to push the child too fast, as this may result in the habituation of faulty learning responses as the student attempts to meet the expectations of parents, teachers, and peers.

We need to find out where the child breaks down in the learning process and understand how a perceptual, memory, or language disability, for example, could interfere with other areas of learning. Learning is a multi-dimensional phenomenon. It is important to understand the relationships between the various processing areas and how they function with each other to enable a child to learn a given task. The teacher needs to ask the right questions, such as: "What kinds of problems does the child have?" "To which areas do I need to give priority in terms of where and how to begin to teach?" The answers to these questions will aid the teacher in determining the rate of input, the amount of input, and the sequence of input for each student. This, in effect, is individualizing instruction for the student who has learning deficits.

The approach to teaching children in this manner can be called *eclectic* in that it pulls together the best of all available resources. It can also be described as *humanistic* in that it emphasizes success even to the extent that in learning, the student shall not experience a failure. The teacher, after reaching a point of failure in instruction, must then drop down to the last success and leave the child with a successful achievement or an accurate model. This approach is humane in that it attempts to change the life style of children who have been failures in school and who have become "failure-avoiding" in their attitude toward learning to one of "success-striving."

It is *behavioristic* and even *atomistic* to the extent that analyzing behavior in the total environment to include material as well as the physical setting is imperative to the development of appropriate educational strategies for particular children.

Principle of "Plateau"

The principle of "plateau" implies that the student shall not remain at the same level of skill development for an extended period of time, without justifiable explanation. Success must become continual for students who have been accustomed to failure. This can be achieved by teachers who escape from the bonds of traditional or prescribed curriculum methodologies and adjust the rate, amount, and sequence of input according to the needs of each student.

Rate of Input

It is essential that the teacher determine the rate of input that is appropriate for each learner. Some children are "slow learners." They need more time for acquiring a skill and are often penalized by timed tests. By trying to go too fast, the teacher may produce anxiety and frustration in these children. Many teachers have a tendency to speed up the rate of input in an attempt to follow the textbook. Unfortunately, most authors, too, do not take into consideration the child who has a slower rate of learning when developing materials for use in schools. A more moderate rate would permit redundancy and repetition that tends to better stabilize that which has been learned. Learning is more efficient when new material is tied in associatively to that which has already been retained. This is especially true for students who exhibit learning difficulties.

Amount of Input

Many children are "jammed" by too much input given at one time. Sometimes that extra spelling word or that extra arithmetic problem may cause the child to forget much of what has already been taught. In controlling the amount of input, the teacher must be careful to leave the child with a successful experience. The key words in leaving children with success are "show me," "give me," "tell me." In this way, they can more readily correct their own errors. Self-correction of errors is a more efficient learning technique than merely listening to the right answer given by another child.

Sequence of Input

One of the critical variables in terms of input is the order of presentation. The teacher must identify the "open channel," that is, the *modality* (auditory, visual, or tactual) which enables the child to learn best. By utilizing the open channels, the teacher can then relate instruction associatively. For example, a child with a visual channel problem may learn best through an auditory-to-visual-plus-tactual association rather than by a visual-to-auditory association. The child who has difficulty learning how to hold a pencil by observing the teacher demonstrating a series of actions may learn best by listening to the teacher describe the action with his eyes shut as she molds his hand around the pencil. He can then visualize the sequence in his mind's eye. The following input sequence is recommended for specific channel deficits:

The Recommended Sequence in Teaching

1. *Auditory Channel Problems*
   (sensory, perception, memory, language)
   Visual⟶Auditory plus Tactual Kinesthetic,
   if necessary

   $(V \longrightarrow A + TK)$

2. *Visual Channel Problems*
   (sensory, perception, memory, language)
   Auditory⟶Visual plus Tactual Kinesthetic,
   if necessary

   $(A \longrightarrow V + TK)$

CHAP. 1   Theoretical Perspectives

3. *Visual and Auditory Channel Problems*
(sensory, perception, memory, language)
Visual⟶Auditory plus Tactual Kinesthetic,
automatically included
(V⟶A⟶T⟶K)

Multi-Setting Applicability

The diagnostic-teaching approach to meeting the needs of learning handicapped children lends itself to implementation in many different educational settings. Traditional as well as open school settings can readily adapt the diagnostic-teaching techniques as long as the basic philosophy of the school incorporates the principle of meeting the needs of individual children, or more specifically, the individualization of instruction. A school modern in physical facility only, that concerns itself primarily with the "learners" omitting the atypical child from the mainstream of education, is a lesser educational program than a one room red brick schoolhouse where the teacher develops appropriate educational programs for all students, including the learning handicapped.

Summary

The three important variables that must be considered where learning problem children are concerned are:

1. The rate of input—how fast?
2. The amount of input—how much?
3. The sequence of input—in what order?

   Primarily, this book is concerned with determining through task analysis what it is that children need to have in order to succeed in school academically. By delineating the critical skills necessary for success in the academic areas of reading, writing, spelling, and arithmetic, the teacher can then identify deficits in children in the language areas which prevent them from succeeding at these tasks. This criterion referenced approach to assessment and curriculum has been proven successful in many educational settings.

EXPLANATION OF DESIGN OF LEARNING CORRELATES

Figure 1.1 depicts the learning design and the important parameters that pertain to the learning patterns of children. It provides the teacher with a framework within which to identify strengths and weaknesses in the learning processes. After identifying these learning correlates as they pertain to particular children, specific educational strategies can then be developed for each child.

II. VERBAL LEARNING SYSTEMS

Perception	Imagery	Language
Discrimination	Memory	Meaning

Conceptualization

Motivational & emotional

Controls

Distractability
Perseveration
Disinhibition
Hyperactivity
Overstimulation
Inhibiting responses
Understimulation

II. NON-VERBAL LEARNING SYSTEMS

Social perception	Imagery	Symbolization

Specific non-verbal functions

Body image
Spatial and temporal orientation
Laterality and directionality

Motor

Gross
Fine

Sensation

III. Visual
Auditory
Tactual-kinesthetic
Olfactory
Gustatory

Key:
Shaded areas represent greater overlap:
I. Level of learning
II. Type of learning
III. Learning channel

FIGURE 1.1 Design of Correlates for Diagnosis and Amelioration of Learning Problems in Children

CHAP. 1   Theoretical Perspectives

VERBAL LEARNING SYSTEMS

Most of what occurs in school can be termed *verbal learning*. By this, we mean speech, reading, writing, and arithmetic. We are concerned in verbal learning with the child's ability to deal with symbols at different levels.

Sensation

The teacher must determine early in the school year whether the learners are able to see or hear (acuity). This can be done through tests of hearing and visual acuity or by merely lining the children up at the back of the room and asking them to respond to their names (auditory) or to symbols on the chalkboard in the teacher's everyday writing (visual). The student who cannot respond appropriately should be referred for further evaluation. Ocular motor or other disorders of vision other than acuity may also affect learning.

The tactual (touch), olfactory (smell), and gustatory (taste) modalities can be used in teaching. The teacher should determine whether or not the child can acquire accurate information through haptic processes. This can be done by experimenting with the child's ability to identify different textures sight unseen. He should be able to describe familiar objects just by touching them and be able to ascertain whether their textures are different or similar. Sensation is the most primitive level of learning and should be considered in all cases where children react atypically to auditory or visual stimuli.

AUDITORY ACUITY. Sometimes the most obvious problem is overlooked in our attempt to seek complex reasons for learning failure. The student with an auditory acuity problem may exhibit any or all of the following:

1. He may be restless and exhibit poor behavior, often disturbing other children in his attempt to get the information he missed.
2. He may have difficulty in following directions and ask for repetitions from the teacher and others. (Check auditory memory.)
3. He could miss a great deal if the teacher speaks while facing the chalkboard, or if he sits in the back of the room.

It is important to note that even a minor uncorrected hearing loss may be a problem if the child is seated too far away from the teacher or with his better ear facing the wall. If the teacher will line up all the children at the back of the room at the beginning of the school year and call their names in his usual voice, he will quickly identify those who cannot hear him from the rear of the room. Further evaluation and referral may save a student from a great deal of frustration. Some students may have hearing aids but refuse to wear them for cosmetic reasons.

VISUAL ACUITY. There are a number of visual disabilities which a teacher should be aware of in handling a problem learner.

Verbal Learning Systems

1. He may exhibit difficulty with near- or far-point vision.
2. Suppression of vision may be present where the bad eye interferes with the good eye causing the child to see a double image. Check unusual head tilt in reading.
3. Convergence difficulties may result from muscle imbalance in that the student cannot focus on a given task for a period of time.
4. Scanning or ocular pursuit problems may interfere with visual tracking and reading.
5. The following signs need special attention as well:
    blinking,
    crossed eyes,
    unusual head tilt,
    tearing, redness, or inflammation of the eye,
    easily fatigued.

Perception

In viewing perception, we are leaving the realm of essentially the senses and entering into processes that can be called more succinctly brain function. In the area of perception, we are concerned with the sub-categories of:

1. *Discrimination:* seeing or hearing likenesses and differences in sounds and symbols.
2. *Figure ground:* the ability to separate what one wishes to attend to visually or auditorially from the surrounding environment.
3. *Localization and attention:* the ability to locate and attend to stimuli in one's environment.
4. *Closure:* the ability to synthesize sounds and symbols or go from the parts to the whole. (In reading, this would be called blending.)

AUDITORY DISCRIMINATION. A student may be unable to hear fine consonant sound discriminations. This may be evident by his inability to differentiate the following:

1. sounds: *f–v, p–b, t–d.*
2. vowels or consonants in spelling, he may omit these in words—for example, he may spell *varnish* as *vrnsh*. (Check visual memory.)
3. similarities in sounds within a word (cannot discriminate that the *and* in *hand* or *sand* are the same sounds)
4. similar beginning or ending sounds in words, such as *man–mat* or *pant–rat*
5. short vowel sounds, such as the *i* in the word *bit* or the *e* in the word *bet*.
6. the second consonant in consonant clusters, such as the *l* in *fl* or the *t* in *st*.
7. the quiet consonant, dropping it in blends and in spelling words like *rust—rut*.

VISUAL DISCRIMINATION. The student may be unable to distinguish fine differences between letters such as *n* and *h*, and, therefore, fail to note other details of words such as *snip* and *ship* or *red* and *rod*. Some children "look too quickly." The teacher should be aware of a

CHAP. 1   Theoretical Perspectives

child's "rate of perception." This can be picked up on timed tests where he may be accurate as far as he goes but finishes well below the average on the final score. Some students with this difficulty may not be able to match letters accurately. The student who has a slower than average rate of perception will need to spend longer time reading material. He should start a few minutes ahead of the group.

AUDITORY FIGURE-GROUND. The student with auditory figure-ground difficulty may exhibit forced attention to noises or sound in his environment. He may attend to irrelevant sounds and may not be able to concentrate on the task at hand or to the speech of others. It has been said that "he hears too well." An example would be the student who hears the police siren or fire engines long before anyone else does. One student stated that he could not concentrate on what the teacher was saying with the other children sharpening pencils and shuffling their feet. Appropriate seating and a reduced auditory stimulus environment should be considered in setting up a program for these children.

VISUAL FIGURE-GROUND. A student who is unable to distinguish an object from the general irrelevant stimuli in the background, and finds it difficult to hold an image while scanning the total pattern may have a visual figure-ground disability. He may lose his place in the book easily or skip sections of a test. He may not complete material presented on a crowded paper. (Quite often publishers of books or workbooks put so much on a page they have to reduce the size of the print and, for example, leave very few "white spaces" in which children may write.) Material that is too colorful or distracting should be avoided for this type of child. The chief complaint from teachers is that "he never finishes his work."

AUDITORY LOCALIZATION AND ATTENTION. Auditory localization and attention is a condition in which a student may have difficulty in locating the source and direction of sound. Some teachers put their desks in the rear of the room and sometimes give instructions from behind children. In order to attend better, the child with a localization problem must first locate the source of sound. Attention may be affected by excessive auditory and/or visual stimuli in the environment. Anxiety will also affect attention.

AUDITORY CLOSURE (BLENDING). Sometimes a student may be unable to break a word into syllables or individual sounds and blend them back into a word. An example of this type of problem with synthesis is the inability to form *cat* from c a t.

VISUAL CLOSURE. A student may have problems with retaining a visual image of a whole word. If given the word in parts as in a puzzle, he may be unable to put it together again correctly. This becomes a problem when teachers attempt to teach blending using letters printed in the center of cards like this: [a][n] instead of using letters printed like this: [a] [n] on cards.

10

Verbal Learning Systems

OBJECT RECOGNITION. Children with difficulties in recognizing an object cannot efficiently integrate visual stimuli into a uniform whole. This is also known as central blindness. Their attention is drawn to the parts rather than to the entire configuration.

Imagery

Imagery involves overall memory whereby the learner is required to remember that which he had heard, seen, or felt. It also involves retaining auditory, visual, and tactual stimuli in sequence. Memory entails both long term and short term processes. Other aspects of memory which are also related to language association functions are called auditory-to-auditory associations and auditory-to-visual associations. The former is the ability to relate a sound to a sound such as knowing, for example, that the sound "m" in man is the same as the sound "m" in map and the latter a sound to a symbol such as relating the sound "m" to the symbol "m".

AUDITORY IMAGERY (MEMORY). A student may have difficulty with the rhyme of word sounds. He may be unable to hear one word and think of another word with the same ending. For example, I give you *mouse* and you give me *house*. This difficulty may display itself in associating a letter with its sound or auditory referent. Watching a child to see if he can associate the sound "m" with the symbol "m," for instance, also may reveal an auditory language association problem. This inability may be evident in bizarre spelling patterns such as writing letters randomly for words or just one word for everything (say, "cat" for each word given on a spelling test). The more technical description of this is to refer to it as an inability to form phoneme-grapheme relationships.

A student may have problems in drawing auditory to visual relationships. One way of testing for this disability is to see if given the sounds tap-tap-tap, a student would be able to draw the right amounts of dots, . . ., or the numeral 3. In this regard, it is also important to check auditory language association.

A student may exhibit difficulty with remembering the sounds of letters given orally. He may be unable to remember the sequence of sounds in a word.

VISUAL IMAGERY (MEMORY) OR MEMORY-SEQUENCE. The student may be able to remember the letters of a word, but not the visual sequence so that a simple word can be misspelled several different ways, sometimes on the same paper. For example, he may write — the word *not* — *ont* or *ton* (a *variable response*), or he may spell the word *not, ont* consistently (a *fixed response*). It appears easier to remediate a variable response than a fixed response whereby the student has stabilized an incorrect pattern. Even though he may know a word in context, when it is presented in a new situation, he thinks he has never seen it before. Some students exhibit reversals in reading and writing such as confusing *b* for *d* and *was* for *saw*. Inversions such as *m* for *w* can be observed when *me* and *we* are taught together. When writing, the student may either forget to punctuate, or he may make odd punctuation marks. For example, he may write $ for? or he may write ₴ for ?. Sometimes when writing sentences, he may use capital letters in the middle of a sentence. When these reversals occur it is a good idea to check visual discrimination as a possible causitive factor.

CHAP. 1   Theoretical Perspectives

Symbolization (Language)

In the area of language, we are concerned with whether or not the individual can apply meaning to words based on his experiences. Is he just a word caller? Is the student able to express himself meaningfully and sequentially? Does he have a speech impediment such as an articulation defect or a stuttering pattern?

RECEPTIVE LANGUAGE. Good receptive ability enables the student to relate speech and words to meaning; he not only can hear and see but can also understand words. Students with receptive problems may not be able to relate spoken or written words to the appropriate unit of experience. An example would be a difficulty in relating the word "bridge" to the concrete object. He may be frustrated in conversation and not be able to understand at a fairly rapid rate of input. Essentially, the student may not be able to "decode" input coming in visually and auditorially at a normal rate. The more specific problem areas under language receptivity are:

1. *Visual language classification*. The student with difficulty in this area often cannot understand difference and sameness by category classification of objects presented visually. For example, when the student is shown a picture of a car and asked whether it belongs with a picture of a pen, knife, hat, or a truck, he cannot discern the correct classification. In this case, it is vehicles or transportation; therefore, car belongs with truck.
2. *Visual language association*. The student with difficulty in this area is unable to understand non-categorical relationships between objects presented to him visually. For example, when the student is shown a picture of a dog and asked whether it belongs with a picture of a bone, car, hat, or a crayon, he cannot discern the correct classification. In this case, dog is associated with bone.
3. *Auditory language classification*. The student with problems in this area often cannot understand difference and sameness by category classification of objects presented orally. For example, when a student is asked whether a boy belongs with a lamp, dress, man, or a door, he cannot discern the correct classification of boy belonging with man.
4. *Auditory language association*. The student who exhibits difficulty in this area is unable to understand non-categorical relationships between words presented orally. For example, when the student is asked whether an oar belongs with a door, sky, lamp, or a boat, he cannot discern the correct association of oar with boat.

EXPRESSIVE LANGUAGE. The student should be able to use words that describe, show action, or characterize. In speech, his verbal expressions may be unclear, unintelligible, and nonsequential involving a great deal of gesturing and pantomiming. He may have difficulty retrieving words or performing the motor act of speech.

Motor Language Expression
1. *Manual language expression*. The student with difficulty in manual expression may be unable to discern the function of an object even though when asked, he may be able to identify it from among other objects. For example, the student may be able to identify a spoon from among other objects but be unable to show you what to do with it manually.
2. *Speech*. The student may exhibit poor speech patterns. He may have difficulties articu-

lating, omit initial, medial, or final sounds, substitute (wabbit for rabbit), distort (lisp, sloppy "s", or hissing), or add (sumber for summer) sounds to words.

Verbal language expression.
The student exhibiting this disorder may be able to identify a pencil from among other objects presented visually. He may be able to show you what can be done with it, but is unable to talk about it in a meaningful way or describe its function. He may have problems with retrieving words for speaking. Verbal expression disorders include syntax and formulation problems which are characterized by difficulty with the smooth and natural flow of the English language. He may be unable to structure his thoughts into grammatically correct verbal units or sentences.

INNER-LANGUAGE. Inner-language is the language with which one thinks. Inner-language serves to integrate experiences associated with a native spoken language. This can also be thought of as *inner-speech*. Inner-speech, in this sense, relates to thinking, while outer or external speech serves to provide for communication between people.

A child who reads well may not necessarily be able to understand the meaning of what he reads. Some children find it difficult to transform experiences into symbols. Students speaking English as their second language often think in their native tongue. Difficulty may arise in their trying to take an examination in English while attempting to think out the problems in Spanish, for example. Inner-language conflict may result from the unwillingness of a child to give up his native language or dialect for standard English.

NON-VERBAL LEARNING SYSTEMS

Social Perception

Some children have difficulty in gleaning meaning from gestures and expressions or from what others may feel to be easily discernable cause—effect relationships. They are unable to understand the significance of the behavior of others and, in some cases, appear to be emotionally disturbed or to exhibit strange behavior patterns.

Imagery

Imagery refers to an ability to recall places or events that do not involve symbols such as how something looks or sounds as part of an experience. The student may not be able to describe his visit to the circus or the way his room looks.

Symbolization

Non-verbal Symbolic Language used in this context refers to deriving meaning from symbols other than words. Students with difficulty in this area have problems with assigning meaning to such non-verbal, abstract things as art, religion, music, holidays, or patriotism. There is a language of art and music from which the individual cannot derive meaning. It appears that

CHAP. 1   Theoretical Perspectives

this disorder is sometimes accompanied by problems in the spatial area such as having difficulty in understanding measurement and exhibiting a poor sense of direction.

Specific Non-verbal Functions

Spatial readiness has been considered by many to be one of the prerequisites for many of the task level academic functions that we call reading, writing, and arithmetic. A good *body image* enables the child to relate himself to his environment. Adequate *spatial–temporal* orientation appears to be important to arithmetical operations and in learning to tell time. Non-verbal aspects of learning that have been recognized as important are the relationships of *spatial-temporal orientation, laterality,* and *directionality* or *left-right orientation* to verbal learning.

BODY IMAGE. Children with poor body image often indicate this in their human figure drawings. Ruling out retardation as a reason for poor performance, they tend to draw distorted or asymmetrical figures, for example, feet coming out of the head or facial features in the wrong places. This may be due to a child's unfamiliarity with the locations of different parts of his body. He may not be able to organize himself physically for a task and may exhibit concomitant difficulties with spatial concepts.

SPATIAL—TEMPORAL ORIENTATION. The student with spatial–temporal difficulties may have problems in understanding such concepts as before, after, left, right, or even simple words such as in and out. Sometimes reversals of letters and numerals are evident along with difficulties in doing arithmetical operations beyond rote memory. The student may exhibit poor alignment of numerals and inadequate spacing in writing. Watch for the student whose number alignment is erratic on such activities as numbering for a spelling test. Difficulty may be noted in understanding measurements, maps, and graphs; the student may have a poor sense of direction. Learning how to tell time is often a problem for children with spatial-temporal difficulties.

LATERALITY AND DIRECTIONALITY. Laterality, or sidedness which is not established, may be evident in a child who cannot relate himself physically to an object in space. He may not be able to tell how far or how near something is in relation to himself. Directionality problems are manifested by poor left–right orientation and also pertains to making spatial judgements about object to object relationships in space.

Motor

Teachers have become more aware recently of the importance of gross and fine motor efficiency in teaching handwriting as well as for many other motor activities that are required in school. It is also apparent that the clumsy or awkward child often becomes socially unacceptable to his parents, his teachers, and his peers.

GROSS MOTOR. The student may exhibit poor coordination, clumsiness, and general difficulty with large muscle activities required in sports.

1. *Balance and coordination.* Children who exhibit balance and coordination problems have difficulty in using both sides of the body simultaneously, individually, or alternately. Poor coordination may affect self-concept as well as inhibit participation in motor activities.
2. *Body rhythm.* A student with body-rhythm difficulty may not be able to perform body rhythms to music or use band instruments effectively. He may have a dysrhythmic walk which often accompanies coordination difficulties.

FINE MOTOR (EYE—HAND COORDINATION). The student may not be able to coordinate eye and hand movements to achieve a specific task. Handwriting as well as other activities that involve fine movement such as sorting or sewing may be poor.

FINE MUSCLE (FINGER STRENGTH). The student may lack the finger strength required to grasp a pencil or to hold an object. However, this may be maturational in young children.

CONCEPTUALIZATION

Conceptualization, or how a child thinks, is dependent upon the integrity of all the previously mentioned levels of learning. The teacher will need to determine at what conceptual level the child is basically functioning. An example of different levels of responses based on concept development is as follows:

Concrete-Level Response
An apple and an orange are both round.
Functional-Level Response
An apple and an orange can both be eaten.
Abstract-Level Response
An apple and an orange are both fruit.

By determining the primary response level of the child, the teacher will be able to select material that is appropriate to the concept level of a particular student. The teacher may need to build classification-type activities into the curriculum where children can be taught to see relationships through the understanding of the concepts of "difference" and "sameness." It is important that children be asked to express themselves verbally in terms of how things are different or the same. It is through verbal expression that the teacher can determine how the child thinks. This will enable the teacher to relate this information to the concept level of the material that is to be learned. The developmental process in learning is speech or verbal efficiency, then reading and writing. Writing is a higher level language function.

CHAP. 1 Theoretical Perspectives

MOTIVATIONAL AND EMOTIONAL FACTORS

The will to learn permeates every process area previously mentioned. A child with a learning problem who appears to be well adjusted may have an emotional problem. The atypical or inefficient learner in our society is considered by many to be a social outcast. Success in school requires that children attain the basic skills of reading, writing, and arithmetic. Failure in acquiring these skills will, in most instances, result in a child who is unhappy about his inability to learn and is unable to function usefully within a progressive adult society.

The teacher must understand that a failure to learn could be due to a combination of processing deficits and could also be accompanied by an unwillingness to learn. Learning requires that many processes function in concert with each other. Educators, of necessity, must concern themselves with the effect of one system on all of the others.

CONTROLS

Other factors that affect learning are associated with the child's inability to cope with school as it is presently set up. He may be easily *distracted* due to stimuli that may be excessive for him. He may be unable to use his "stop and go mechanism" or controls efficiently, resulting in *perseverative* behavior. Some children are carried away by their own thoughts and give inappropriate responses to questions. This is sometimes called *disinhibited* behavior. Others are *hyperactive* due to organic disorders. Frustration with teachers or the inability to cope with the way the task is presented often results in *aggression*. Children who are *overstimulated* find it difficult to attend to the task or even retain that which has been taught. Children who spend most of their time *inhibiting* their own behavior due to pressures of one kind or another sometimes have little energy left for learning. There are other children, however, who do not receive enough stimulation. These *understimulated* children need an environment that will challenge their abilities.

The chapters that follow include developmental inventories, screening tests, and additional suggestions for both formal and informal evaluation. This assessment information along with an array of educational strategies in the language arts area and in arithmetic should give the classroom teacher and other professionals a basic fund of educational techniques necessary for meeting the needs of children who manifest a variety of learning disabilities.

CHAPTER 2

DEVELOPMENTAL SPELLING INVENTORIES

SCREENING USING A SPELLING INVENTORY

A spelling inventory can be used for individual assessment or as an aid in determining the range of reading abilities and possible deficit areas in learning of a large group of students. Children who have difficulty in reading, as a rule, have difficulty in spelling. An inventory can be made up of words taken from the basal spelling series used in the school.

The developmental spelling inventory serves two purposes:

1. The spelling errors can be diagnostic in that they indicate the weaker channel for learning by the nature of the mistakes made. The type of errors made will suggest to the teacher the areas of learning that need to be further explored. Spelling inventory screening as a formal means of evaluation will either support or negate the judgments teachers make on the basis of informal observation.
2. Such a spelling inventory enables the teacher to determine at which point screening with developmental reading inventories ought to begin. With this in mind, the teacher should begin one level below that at which the student failed in spelling to test for reading ability. This will reduce the degree of failure for some children and also identify quickly the more advanced learners in the class.

DEVELOPING A SPELLING INVENTORY

The procedure for making a spelling inventory is a simple one. Below are the directions for setting up such a test:

1. Select a word sample from each basal spelling book of a given spelling series.
2. Take fifteen words from the grade one speller.
3. Take twenty words from the grades two through six spellers.

CHAP. 2   Developmental Spelling Inventories

Note: To take a sample selection from grades two through six divide the number of words listed at the back of the spelling book by twenty. If there are 300 words in the book, you would divide 300 by twenty giving you fifteen. Therefore, a word sample would consist of every fifteenth word in the speller. Should you decide not to develop your own inventory, you could use the Mann-Suiter Developmental Spelling Inventory which can be found on page 19.

SCREENING PROCEDURES

For grade four and below, begin testing by administering first-level spelling words. For fifth grade and above, begin testing with the third-level spelling words. Thus, for children who fail the third level, there always remains a second level to which they can be dropped. In giving the test the teacher should (1) say the word, (2) use the word in a sentence, and then (3) repeat the word again. It is important that the teacher stress to the students that even if they cannot spell a word, they should put down every sound they can think of in the word. If, for example, the teacher is screening a fourth grade class, he should dictate words from the levels one and two lists at the first sitting and then check the responses. At the second sitting, he should test only those students who were able to successfully spell the words given at the first sitting since there is no sense in testing those who have already failed the first two levels. To avoid continued frustration a child who misses seven words at a level—which constitutes failure at that level—should not be tested any further. At the third sitting, the teacher should finish screening only those students who were successful with the previous words.

SPELLING ERRORS TO LOOK FOR

Spelling Errors Primarily Due to Auditory-Channel Deficits

1. Substitutes *t* for *d*, *f* for *v*, *sh* for *ch*. (auditory discrimination or cultural)
2. Does not hear subtle differences in or discriminate between sounds and often leaves vowels out of two syllable words such as spelling *plsh* for *polish*. (Auditory acuity and/or discrimination)
3. Discerns the beginning or ending of a word but not the middle of the word which may be missing or usually wrong such as spelling *h--d* for *hand*. (Auditory acuity and/or discrimination)
4. Confuses vowels such as spelling the word *bit* as *bet*. (Auditory discrimination)
5. Omits the second letter in blends spelling *fled* as *fed*. (Auditory acuity and/or discrimination)
6. Uses a synonym such as *house* for *home* in spelling. (Auditory–visual association)
7. Omits word endings such as *ed, s,* or *ing*. (Cultural or auditory discrimination)
8. Takes wild guesses with little or no relationship between the letters or words used and the spelling words dictated, such as spelling *dog* for *home*. (Auditory–visual associative memory)

Spelling Errors To Look For

FIGURE 2.1 Mann-Suiter Developmental Spelling Inventory

Level I	Level II	Level III
1. cat	1. nod	1. sheep
2. no	2. jug	2. each
3. red	3. get	3. third
4. see	4. sip	4. catch
5. and	5. tab	5. drank
6. you	6. sled	6. lake
7. the	7. clap	7. stick
8. we	8. ship	8. duck
9. it	9. drop	9. child
10. yes	10. think	10. bath
11. dog	11. sing	11. wash
12. big	12. little	12. puppy
13. like	13. home	13. train
14. have	14. ask	14. laughing
15. was	15. father	15. short
	16. doll	16. swing
	17. morning	17. walk
	18. pretty	18. uncle
	19. boat	19. right
	20. said	20. because

Level IV	Level V	Level VI
1. strike	1. ridge	1. scene
2. shook	2. frame	2. court
3. choke	3. risky	3. relation
4. hobby	4. quietly	4. noble
5. chopped	5. ditch	5. maples
6. swimming	6. trouble	6. describe
7. hiding	7. address	7. enforce
8. folded	8. heroes	8. motoring
9. studies	9. soldiers	9. relieves
10. doesn't	10. thieves	10. autograph
11. through	11. crept	11. canyon
12. climb	12. movies	12. glistening
13. listen	13. studying	13. continued
14. person	14. joking	14. trophy
15. pennies	15. ruins	15. pierced
16. ashes	16. reviewed	16. motoring
17. starting	17. sauce	17. whirl
18. age	18. business	18. ignorantly
19. dirty	19. expect	19. hastened
20. carrying	20. dismissed	20. rewarded

Note: Children can usually spell only words they can read; therefore, by adding up the correct words on each paper and then placing the papers in an order from low to high, the teacher will have an immediate idea of the relative reading levels of the students. Spelling screens should occasionally be given on unlined white paper. This will give the teacher a sample of the student's handwriting which can be analyzed for good spacing, letter production, and positioning of words on a page.

CHAP. 2   Developmental Spelling Inventories

After screening the students with the developmental spelling inventory, the teacher can start testing for reading abilities. Testing for reading should begin with the students who made the lowest scores on the spelling inventory since they are the children who will need a more accurate and comprehensive analysis of reading abilities.

It is suggested that in testing for reading with the DWRI (Developmental Word Reading Inventory, Chapter 3) that the teacher begin the evaluation by dropping down to one level below the student's last successful level in spelling. However, should the student not be able to spell at all, then the following readiness skills should be assessed:

1. Does he know the letter names and sounds?
2. Can he match a letter sound with its visual symbol?
3. Can he match a letter name with its visual symbol?

Spelling Errors Primarily Due to Visual Channel Deficits

1. Visualizes the beginning or the ending of words but omits the middle of the word such as spelling *hapy* for *happy*. (Visual memory.)
2. Gives the correct letters but in the wrong sequence. The word *the* may be written as *teh* or *hte*. (Visual-memory sequence.)
3. Reverses letters or words such as writing **2** for *s*, *b* for *d*, *on* for *no*, or *was* for *saw*.
4. Inverts letters such as writing *u* for *n*, *m* for *w*. (Usually visual memory but could also be either visual discrimination or spatial.)
5. Mixes up capitals and small letters—cAt. This is also evident in cursive writing. (Poor transitional teaching or visual memory.)

Note: Sometimes mixing of capitals and small letters is due to the student attempting to compensate for not knowing the small letters by substituting capital letters for the small letter he has not learned.

MANN-SUITER DEVELOPMENTAL SPELLING INVENTORY

The Mann-Suiter Developmental Spelling Inventory is comprised of samples of several basal and linguistic spelling lists (Figure 2.1) These lists represent different spelling programs. They have been both randomly selected according to level of difficulty and general orientation and stratified in order to achieve a balance in terms of different spelling patterns, prefixes and suffixes, and configurations of words. Trial testing involved approximately 250 students, grades 1 through 6. Their performances were compared to the level of their functioning as indicated by teachers. In approximately 80% of the cases there was agreement in comparing teacher estimates of student performance and student achievement on the Mann-Suiter Developmental Spelling Inventory.

CHAPTER 3

DEVELOPMENTAL READING INVENTORIES

The previous chapter discussed the methods related to the Mann-Suiter inventory of students' spelling capabilities as a basal measurement procedure for the language arts. This chapter will provide specific suggestions for the formation and use of developmental reading inventories. The purposes of the Developmental Reading Inventories are:

1. To aid the teacher in determining the three levels of reading which have been traditionally defined as "independent," "instructional," and "frustration" levels.
2. To provide the teacher with information at the task level in the language arts area as well as to point out possible deficits that result in failure in reading.
3. To indicate the students' strengths and weaknesses by analyzing their performance at the reading task. The results of these tests can become the basis for selecting appropriate educational strategies for particular children.

There will be two forms of reading assessment delineated in this chapter: (1) teacher developed inventories based on the available language arts series, and (2) the Mann-Suiter Developmental Reading Inventories.

DEVELOPING A WORD READING INVENTORY

In developing a word reading inventory, the teacher begins by taking a sample of words from the back of basal reading books of various grade levels. He selects a word sample of fifteen words at the PP3 level (approximately, every second or third word). The formula for extracting these words is similar to that described for the Mann-Suiter spelling inventory. For all other grade levels the teacher picks a sample of twenty words, dividing the number of words in the book by twenty. Say there are 200 new words in the book, 200 divided by twenty would give ten; therefore, a sample selection would be every tenth word from the list

FIGURE 3.1 Teacher's Developmental Word-Recognition Scoring Sheet

NAME _____ DATE _____

✓ = Correct   ✓ = Incorrect   Examiner _____

	Pre-Primer				Primer	
	Flash	Stimulus	Untimed		Flash	Stimulus	Untimed
1. ___		the	___	1. ___		with	___
2. ___		a	___	2. ___		good	___
3. ___		red	___	3. ___		they	___
4. ___		see	___	4. ___		run	___
5. ___		to	___	5. ___		girl	___
6. ___		house	___	6. ___		all	___
7. ___		said	___	7. ___		duck	___
8. ___		little	___	8. ___		this	___
9. ___		big	___	9. ___		yellow	___
10. ___		not	___	10. ___		away	___
11. ___		ball	___	11. ___		home	___
12. ___		get	___	12. ___		are	___
13. ___		I	___	13. ___		but	___
14. ___		in	___	14. ___		he	___
15. ___		want	___	15. ___		like	___
				16. ___		my	___
___		Errors	___	17. ___		that	___
___		Score	___	18. ___		one	___
6½ points each				19. ___		went	___
Observations:				20. ___		will	___
_____				___		Errors	___
				___		Score	___
						5 points each	

22

in the back of the book.) After the words have been selected for each level, it is important that the teacher go back and check and see if he has included the following:

For grade one

1. A variety of vowel and consonant sounds in different positions.
2. Words that are similar and different in configuration (a few words may be exchanged in order to achieve this).

For grades two through six

1. A variety of vowel and consonant sounds in different positions.
2. Words that are similar and different in configuration.
3. Words with prefixes such as *pre* and *re* and suffixes such as *ed* and *ing*.
4. Words which have abstract meanings such as liberty, justice, etc., as language development is also being tested at the same time.

Note: Proper nouns are not included. By convention, they are omitted.

Developing Scoring Sheets

Figure 3.1 illustrates how a teacher's copy of word-recognition scoring sheets can be designed (Johnson and Kress, 1965). After having selected a word sample from the various levels and made some adjustments as recommended (using good judgment), the teacher is now ready to make up his own word-recognition scoring sheets. The words are typed clearly and double spaced on white paper as shown in Figure 3.1. These sheets are to be used only by the teacher and are designed to record each child's responses.

Developing a Tachistoscope

After having selected the vocabulary and made up the score the teacher is ready to construct a device which can be used to present the words to the student. The words should be presented in a manual tachistoscopic fashion. The instructions for making a sample word-recognition tachistoscope are presented in Figure 3.2 (a) and (b). (Durrell 1956)

Note: Primer letter type should be used for word list selections from PP3 through the first level.

MANN-SUITER DEVELOPMENTAL READING INVENTORIES

The Mann-Suiter Developmental Reading Inventory was compiled in the following manner:

1. The word-recognition section was developed by sampling different basal and linguistic word lists. These lists were representative of many different reading programs and were selected according to level of difficulty. Some stratification was accomplished in order to

FIGURE 3.2 (a) Instructions for Constructing a Tachistoscope: The Screen

A tab stapled on top of strip for ease of handling.
All words should be double spaced. Primery letter type should be used
for PP through level one words. Again materials to be considered can be
an oak tag or strips cut from manila folders.

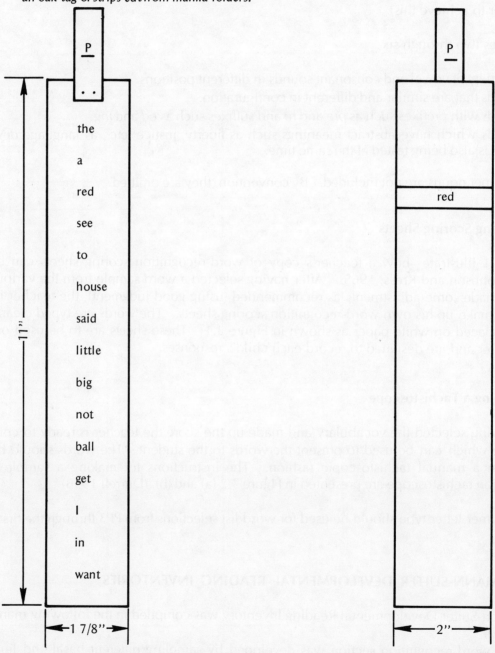

FIGURE 3.2 (b) Instructions for Constructing a Tachistoscope: The Image

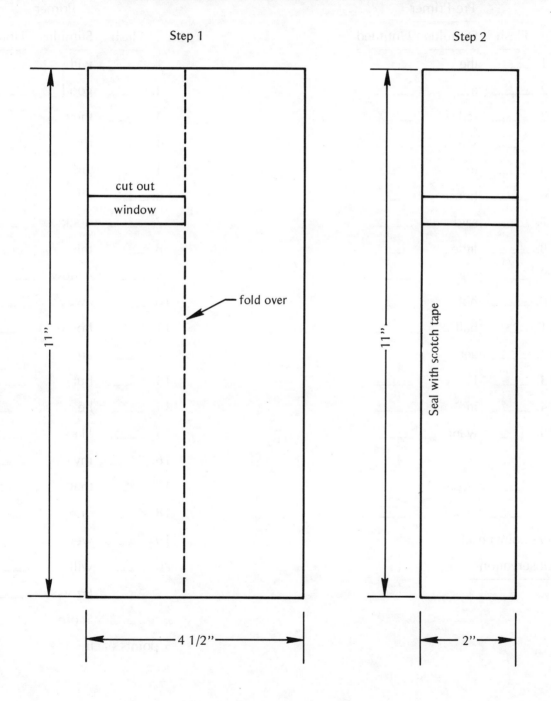

FIGURE 3.3 (a) Mann-Suiter Developmental Word-Recognition Scoring Sheet

NAME _____ DATE _____

✓ = Correct   ✓ = Incorrect   Examiner _____

Pre-Primer

	Flash	Stimulus	Untimed
1.	_____	the	_____
2.	_____	a	_____
3.	_____	red	_____
4.	_____	see	_____
5.	_____	to	_____
6.	_____	house	_____
7.	_____	said	_____
8.	_____	little	_____
9.	_____	big	_____
10.	_____	not	_____
11.	_____	ball	_____
12.	_____	get	_____
13.	_____	I	_____
14.	_____	in	_____
15.	_____	want	_____
	_____	Errors	_____
	_____	Score	_____

6½ points each

Observations:

Primer

	Flash	Stimulus	Untimed
1.	_____	with	_____
2.	_____	good	_____
3.	_____	they	_____
4.	_____	run	_____
5.	_____	girl	_____
6.	_____	all	_____
7.	_____	duck	_____
8.	_____	this	_____
9.	_____	yellow	_____
10.	_____	away	_____
11.	_____	home	_____
12.	_____	are	_____
13.	_____	but	_____
14.	_____	he	_____
15.	_____	like	_____
16.	_____	my	_____
17.	_____	that	_____
18.	_____	one	_____
19.	_____	went	_____
20.	_____	will	_____
	_____	Errors	_____
	_____	Score	_____

5 points each

FIGURE 3.3 (b) Mann-Suiter Developmental Word-Recognition Scoring Sheet

NAME _____ DATE _____

✓ = Correct   ✓ = Incorrect   Examiner _____

	First-Reader Level				Second-Reader Level	
	Flash	Stimulus	Untimed		Flash	Stimulus	Untimed
1.	____	many	____	1.	____	head	____
2.	____	took	____	2.	____	nice	____
3.	____	feet	____	3.	____	room	____
4.	____	way	____	4.	____	string	✓
5.	____	food	____	5.	____	through	____
6.	____	again	____	6.	____	side	____
7.	____	know	____	7.	____	knew	____
8.	____	over	____	8.	____	blew	✓
9.	____	other	____	9.	____	air	____
10.	____	next	____	10.	____	tire	✓
11.	____	please	____	11.	____	strong	____
12.	____	off	____	12.	____	floor	____
13.	____	nests	____	13.	____	wash	____
14.	____	be	____	14.	____	while	____
15.	____	time	____	15.	____	ever	____
16.	____	drop	____	16.	____	both	____
17.	____	thing	____	17.	____	anything	____
18.	____	when	____	18.	____	hard	____
19.	____	their	____	19.	____	beautiful	____
20.	____	frog	____	20.	____	gray	____
	____	Errors	____		____	Errors	____
	____	Scores	____		____	Scores	____

5 points each

5 points each

Observations: _____

FIGURE 3.3 (c) Mann-Suiter Developmental Word-Recognition Scoring Sheet

NAME _____ DATE _____

✓ = Correct   ✓ = Incorrect   Examiner _____

Third-Reader Level

Flash	Stimulus	Untimed
1. ___	nail	___
2. ___	breakfast	___
3. ___	sniff	___
4. ___	great	___
5. ___	eight	___
6. ___	lazy	___
7. ___	fifteen	___
8. ___	since	✓
9. ___	path	___
10. ___	whole	___
11. ___	tribe	✓
12. ___	freeze	___
13. ___	shades	✓
14. ___	gravel	✓
15. ___	awake	___
16. ___	cousin	___
17. ___	journey	✓
18. ___	scatter	___
19. ___	saddle	✓
20. ___	earth	___
___	Errors	
___	Scores	

5 points each

Observations: _____

Fourth-Reader Level

Flash	Stimulus	Untimed
1. ___	spy	✓
2. ___	fortune	✓
3. ___	sheriff	___
4. ___	alive	___
5. ___	glanced	___
6. ___	breathe	✓
7. ___	statement	___
8. ___	design	___
9. ___	pleasant	✓
10. ___	bacon	✓
11. ___	weather	___
12. ___	island	✓
13. ___	west	___
14. ___	success	✓
15. ___	trail	✓
16. ___	leave	✓
17. ___	knowledge	✓
18. ___	peace	___
19. ___	rough	✓
20. ___	guides	✓
___	Errors	
___	Scores	

5 points each

FIGURE 3.3 (d) Mann-Suiter Developmental Word-Recognition Scoring Sheet

NAME _____ DATE _____

✓ = Correct   ✓ = Incorrect   Examiner _____

<u>Fifth-Reader Level</u>   <u>Sixth-Reader Level</u>

	Flash	Stimulus	Untimed		Flash	Stimulus	Untimed
1.	_____	natural	✓	1.	_____	fleet	_____
2.	_____	parents	_____	2.	_____	poisoned	_____
3.	_____	defeat	_____	3.	_____	members	_____
4.	_____	fought	✓	4.	_____	denied	_____
5.	_____	horrible	_____	5.	_____	movie	_____
6.	_____	anger	_____	6.	_____	summoned	_____
7.	_____	regarding	✓	7.	_____	license	_____
8.	_____	leisure	✓	8.	_____	wreath	_____
9.	_____	invitation	_____	9.	_____	liberty	_____
10.	_____	ancient	✓	10.	_____	shifted	_____
11.	_____	delicious	_____	11.	_____	blonde	_____
12.	_____	shrill	✓	12.	_____	abandon	_____
13.	_____	amount	✓	13.	_____	partial	_____
14.	_____	seldom	✓	14.	_____	spoil	_____
15.	_____	guiding	✓	15.	_____	extensive	_____
16.	_____	salmon	✓	16.	_____	unwise	_____
17.	_____	loudly	_____	17.	_____	cooperation	_____
18.	_____	whether	_____	18.	_____	simple	_____
19.	_____	flesh	✓	19.	_____	negative	_____
20.	_____	gurgle	✓	20.	_____	omitted	_____
	_____	Errors	_____		_____	Errors	_____
	_____	Scores	_____		_____	Scores	_____

5 points each   5 points each

Observations: _____

CHAP. 3   Developmental Reading Inventories

achieve a balance in terms of spelling patterns, prefixes and suffixes, and different configurations of words.
2. The Paragraph Reading Inventory is comprised of original stories and developed on the basis of the following formulas: (a) for grades 1 through 3, the George Spache (Spache 1953) formula and (b) for grades 4 through 6, the Dale-Chall (Dale and Chall 1948) formula.

Approximately 375 students, grades 1 through 6, were administered the entire inventory and compared to their level of functioning as specified by teachers. In approximately 85% of the cases there was agreement between the estimates of teachers and the students' performance on the Mann-Suiter Developmental Inventories.

ADMINISTERING DEVELOPMENTAL WORD-RECOGNITION INVENTORY

1. During the test, the teacher should sit opposite the student at a table.
2. The first word should be centered in the window of the tachistoscope but covered with a white unlined 3 × 5 index card. (Variations of presentations to children can be used based on teacher preference.)
3. The teacher should ask the student to watch and then expose the whole word clearly and quickly, making sure the child initially gets only a flash presentation of the word.
4. The timing for the complete movement on the flash showing of the word should be approximately that required to say "one thousand" at a normal rate.

Note: No more than one flash exposure should be given. This means the examiner must *be sure that the child is ready and attending.*

5. If the student responds quickly, the examiner immediately records a check ✓ in the flash response column and goes on to the next word.
6. If, however, the student gives an incorrect response, record a different check ✓ in the flash column and note everything that is said.
7. No clues should be given, but the student should be allowed to re-examine the word and answer if he can. No help should be given. The answer is then recorded in the untimed column.
8. When a student does not know a word, additional information can be obtained by asking him if he knows any part of the word. The teacher can cover part of the word and ask the student if he knows it, and then determine if he can blend the parts. This step is optional but helpful diagnostically.
9. The teacher must record all responses immediately and continue testing until the student misses seven of the twenty words on an untimed section for a particular grade level word selection.

Note: The teacher must remember to cover the teacher scoring sheet with his arm so that the student cannot read the words ahead of time.

Recording Student Responses

The following compilation of commonly used notations will provide teachers with a common language by which they can communicate their findings to each other in a meaningful way:

Scoring of Developmental Word Reading Inventories

Stimulus Word	Notation	
see	✓	indicates a correct response
the	✓ (slashed)	indicates no response or an incorrect response
sun	s-u-n	indicates an attempt to reproduce the word phonetically
at	it/ate	indicates two wrong responses
where	when ✓	indicates corrected wrong first response
that	t/h/a/t	indicates student named the letters he saw but could not say the word or any part of the word.
duck	d k	indicates only what the child said he saw

SCORING OF DEVELOPMENTAL WORD READING INVENTORIES

On the *Developmental Word Reading Inventory,* there is an allowance for a self-correction of errors. A response is counted accurate if

1. on the flash section, the student self-corrects before the untimed exposure (the teacher must be sure to write down the initial response);
2. the student corrects the flash error during the untimed exposure. The error is counted only on the flash section of the test.

Note: There should be two scores obtained from each level test, one representing the student's flash vocabulary and the other his ability to identify words in an untimed fashion.

FIGURE 3.4 Score Chart for Flash and Untimed Words

Pre-Primer	Primer and Above
1 = 94%	1 = 95%
2 = 87%	2 = 90%
3 = 80%	3 = 85%
4 = 74%	4 = 80%
5 = 67%	5 = 75%
6 = 60%	6 = 70%
7 = 54%	7 = 65%
8 = 47%	8 = 60%
9 = 40%	9 = 55%
10 = 34%	10 = 50%

WORD READING ERRORS TO LOOK FOR

Word Reading Errors Primarily Due to Auditory Channel Deficits

1. The student may be able to read letters and give names of letters but be unable to identify

CHAP. 3   Developmental Reading Inventories

the sounds of letters (auditory–visual associative memory and/or auditory discrimination).

2. He may take wild guesses at words with little or no relationship between the word seen and the word called (auditory–visual associative memory).
3. Sometimes a student may substitute a synonym such as *house* for *home* (auditory–visual associative memory).
4. He may substitute one sound for another and read *bit* for *bet* (auditory discrimination).
5. He may know the sounds but still be unable to blend them into words (auditory closure).

Word Reading Errors Primarily Due to Visual Channel Deficits

1. The student may exhibit a slow rate of perception and be unable to read the word when it is flashed but be able to identify the word on the untimed presentation. Time makes the difference (rate of perception).
2. He may discern only the beginning or the ending of a word and lose the middle (visual closure and/or rate of perception).
3. He may reverse the letters in a word, such as *was-saw, on-no* (usually visual memory, check visual discrimination and spatial).
4. He may invert letters, for example, *me* for *we* (usually visual memory, check visual discrimination and spatial).
5. He may fail to discriminate fine differences between letters and read *ship* for *snip* or *red* for *rod* (visual discrimination).
6. He may add sounds to words such as reading *dogs* for *dog* (visual memory and/or misperception).
7. The student may try to sound words phonetically exhibiting excessive hesitations (check visual memory). This can also be indicative of an oral expressive (retrieval) disorder where the student knows the word but cannot retrieve the correct motor sequence.

In administering the Word Reading Inventory the following three pointers need to be kept in mind: (1) What do the errors on the Developmental Spelling Inventory mean diagnostically? (2) Is the student making similar errors on the Developmental Word Reading Inventory? (3) Am I observing the way he reads the words as well as trying to get a measure of his reading level?

CHECKING FOR ORAL LANGUAGE DEVELOPMENT

Additional information can be obtained about the level of a student's word reading ability by testing the student's oral language development according to the following:

1. After having completed a level, the teacher would go back and select three words at random that the student has read successfully and ask him (a) to use the word in a sentence, and (b) to tell what the word means. For example, on the PP3 list, the teacher asked a student to use the word duck in a *sentence*. He did it accurately and S+ was written next to the word on the teacher scoring sheet. If the response had been wrong, the teacher would have marked S– next to the word. The teacher then asked the student the

Checking for Oral Language Development

meaning of the word. The response was correct and therefore, *M+* was written next to the word on the teacher scoring sheet. Had the word been defined incorrectly, the teacher would have written *M−* next to it. Manual expressions of meaning are acceptable but should be noted.

2. Only three words should be used from each selection.
3. The Analysis of Errors Sheets (Chapter 6) contain a section on vocabulary which has been delineated into two basic levels for different grades: Concrete-Functional, or Abstract. The *level of conceptualization* tells us how the student thinks. It is important for the teacher to know at what level the child is basically functioning so that he can plan for an appropriate selection of materials and not overload the student with concepts that are too difficult for him to cope with
   (a) The Concrete-Functional level (*C−F*) is defined as any response that describes the quality, state of being, or function of the object to be defined. An essentially concrete level response would be that an apple is round. A response at the functional level would be that an apple can be eaten.
   (b) The Abstract level (*A*) is defined as any response that indicates a synonym, classification, or association. A more abstract level response would be that an apple is a fruit.

The word meanings for any grade level can be classified according to the above mentioned levels of conceptualization. They can be used in conjunction with the word meanings given in the Developmental Paragraph Reading Inventory, that will follow, to aid the teacher in determining the student's overall level of responses. The teacher can then make the appropriate notation on the Analysis of Error Sheets to be found on page 56.

Observable Behaviors

The following behaviors should be noted on the score sheet if they are present:

1. Tension or nervousness.
2. Easily distracted.
3. Visual difficulties (ocular motor).
4. Hearing difficulties.
5. Speech problems (stuttering, articulation, voice).
6. Bizarre responses.

Testing with the Developmental Paragraph Reading Inventory should continue. Later, the scores on the Developmental Word Recognition Inventory can be plotted on the Developmental Reading Summary to be found on page 41.

Developmental Paragraph Reading Inventory

The teacher can construct a Developmental Paragraph Reading Inventory (DPRI) from any basal reading series available. The DPRI is designed to do the following:

1. Determine the child's independent, instructional, and frustration reading levels.

CHAP. 3 Developmental Reading Inventories

2. Identify specific types of word-recognition errors.
3. Estimate comprehension ability.
4. Determine the extent of the student's vocabulary.
5. Obtain information relative to the child's rate of performance.

DEVELOPING A DEVELOPMENTAL PARAGRAPH READING INVENTORY

1. Select any basal reading series and take a reading selection from the back one third of each of the levels. Be sure to get a representative variety to avoid extreme variations. The following readability formulas will aid you in being more accurate in terms of choosing an appropriate selection: (a) For grades one through three, use the George Spache Formula (Spache 1953); and (b) for grades four through six use the Dale-Chall Formula (Dale and Chall 1948).
2. Begin at the PP3 level and proceed to as high a level as necessary for your class. The chart following (p.35) will help you decide upon the length of the readings to be used, in terms of the number of words in each selection:

FIGURE 3.5 Mann-Suiter Developmental Paragraph Reading Inventory. Sample Teacher Scoring Sheet

MOTIVATIONAL QUESTION: Have you ever seen a red dog? Find out what kind of a dog Jane and Dick saw in this story.

Pre-Primer 3   (29 words — Form A)

THE RED DOG

"Look, look," said Jane.

"See the funny little dog.

Can you see it?

It is red."

"I see it," said Dick.

"It is a toy dog."

Errors:	0	1	2	3	4	5
	100	96	93	89	86	83

Detail   1. What did Jane see? (a funny little dog, a red dog, or a toy dog)
Vocabulary   What does the word "little" mean? (small, etc.)
Main Idea   2. Why did Jane call the little dog funny? (it was red)
Inference   3. Where do you think the children were? (toy store, etc.)
Detail   4. What kind of a dog did Dick say it was? (toy)

Errors:	0	1	2	3
	100	75	50	25

Developing a Developmental Paragraph Reading Inventory

Level	Words (Approximate)	Questions
PP3	20–30	5
P	30–40	5
1	35–50	5
2^1	40–55	5
2^2	45–60	5
3^1	60–90	5
3^2	60–100	5
4	75–125	5
5	90–150	5
6	100–175	5

3. Construct the teacher scoring sheet and the student's reading copy. An example of the teacher's scoring sheet of a PP3 selection is shown in Figure 3.5. The teacher's copy can be dittoed. The student's reading selection can by typed on a sheet of oak tag, on non-glossy white cardboard, heavy white bond paper, or on pieces cut from manila folders.

Student's Copy

```
The Red Dog
_____
_____
_____
_____
```

Hard paper

Use primer type for reading selections PP3 through first level.

Teacher's Scoring Sheet

```
The Red Dog

(score) ..........
1 _____
2 _____
3 _____
4 _____
(score) ..........
```

Ditto

Only the teacher sees the dittoed sheets.

Note: The length of the sentences should be approximately the same length found in the appropriate grade level basal reader.

How to Write Comprehension Questions for the Paragraph Inventory

The order of the type of questions (detail, main idea, vocabulary or inference) should follow the text or sequence of the reading selection and therefore will be different for each story. Comprehension questions should be asked after every reading selection. Good questions can be obtained by using the following outline. The questions should be based upon each selection in the basal reading series that is used. Below is a list of areas the questions should cover.

CHAP. 3   Developmental Reading Inventories

Sample types of questions

1. *Vocabulary Questions.*
   Example:
   a. What does the word ___ mean?
   b. What is another meaning for the word ___?
   c. What is a word that can be used in place of ___?

Note: Look for Concrete-Functional or Abstract Responses.

2. *Detail Questions.* Questions should be included that require the student to tell what something is or is not doing. These questions can describe a quantity, quality, state of being, or an action.
   Example:
   a. What did Jane see?
   b. What color was the dog?
3. *Main Idea Questions.* One question in each selection should reflect the essence of the story or of the main character in the story.
   Example:
   a. Why was Ann excited?
   b. Why did Bill's mother tell him not to go swimming alone?
4. *Inference Questions.* Questions of this nature should require the student to formulate a logical deduction from several bits of available information.
   Example:
   a. What time of day was it? (The story tells about shooting stars.)
   b. How do we know that John was being teased? (The story describes the teasing of a blind boy.)

SCREENING PROCEDURES FOR THE DEVELOPMENTAL PARAGRAPH READING INVENTORY

1. Select a level at which the student can begin with a success before he ultimately fails. You can also begin at the highest level at which the child had 85 to 90% correct on the untimed section of the Developmental Word Reading Inventory.
2. Before he begins, tell him that you will ask him a few questions about the story when he has finished. (Do not allow him to preread the selection silently.)
3. Hand the child the reading selection, read the motivational question to him and ask him to read "out loud" to you. Be sure the student reads the title of each selection.
4. Always ask the questions as soon as the reading is completed, and permit the child to hold on to the selection so that he can refer to it as necessary. We do not want to penalize the student for possible difficulties with memory. However, if unusual amounts of time are used to find information, this should be noted.

Note: If the pupil fails to respond to the teacher's questions appropriately, he may be asked to "explain more fully" or to "tell me more," etc. Although there is a lack of response category on the score sheet to be considered in the total scoring, probing questions are permitted. However, use good judgment in such instances.

Scoring Procedures

Be sure to mark the correct and incorrect responses by each question as it is asked. If there are two or three parts to the answer, give credit for the correct portion answered. For example, "What did Mary do first? Next? And last?" Each part of this question is worth one-third of the credit.

Note: Do not forget to record unusual answers. Customarily, vocabulary questions are never counted into the comprehension score.

SCORING PROCEDURES FOR THE DEVELOPMENTAL PARAGRAPH READING INVENTORY

Symbol Notation

As the child reads the selection, use the following symbols to record the types of word recognition errors made during the paragraph reading selection.

1. *Unusual phrasing, or word-by-word reading.*
   Example: A/ little black dog ran/ away/ from home.
   (Noted but not counted as an error.)
2. *Omitted words, phrases, or word endings.*
   Example: A little black dog ran away from home. He talked (and talked) to her. He talk(s) to her. (Counted as an error.)
3. *Substitutions*
   Example: Mary walked ^above^ over the bridge.
   The teacher writes the substituted word above. (Counted as an error.)
4. *Additions of words, phrases, or endings.*
   Example: A little black dog(gy) ran away from ^the^ home. (Counted as an error.)
5. *Repetitions*
   Example: |A little black dog |ran| away from home. A line is drawn indicating the portion repeated. (Noted but not counted as an error.)
6. *Mispronunciation or words.*
   Write M above the word.
   Example: "The big ^M^ machine." The error is in placing the accent on the wrong syllable. The evaluator should also write out the errors. (Counted as an error.)
7. *Punctuation.*
   The student continues to read through the punctuation marks. Example: A little dog ran away˟He ran, etc. (Noted but not counted as an error.)
8. *Needs assistance.*
   If he hesitates more than five seconds, write P above the word and pronounce it for the student. (Counted as an error.)
9. *Self-correction of errors.*
   Example: She saw ^was✓^ a penny. (Noted but not counted as an error.)
10. *Hesitations.*
    Example: A little black dog ran haway.

CHAP. 3   Developmental Reading Inventories

If the child hesitates noticeably, put an *H* before the word. (Noted but not counted as an error.)

Each of the errors can be scored as indicated. Sometimes the teacher has to use his judgment in scoring. A good rule of thumb is to score anything that changes or distorts the meaning or intent of the selection as an error.

Summary of Word Recognition Errors

The child makes an error when he:

1. Omits a word.
2. Substitutes a word.
3. Adds a word.
4. Mispronounces a word.
5. Asks the examiner to pronounce a word for him.

Note: Proper names are not counted as errors as they depend upon experiential factors.

Scoring of Comprehension Questions

Divide 100 by the number of questions, not including vocabulary questions to get the value of each comprehension question. For example, if the first-level reading selection has 5 questions, including one vocabulary question, you divide 100 by 4 to get the value of each question.

After the teacher obtains the percentage correct from each of the levels tested, the scores should then be recorded on the Developmental Reading Summary Record (Figure 3.6) under Reading-Comprehension. Both the word-recognition and comprehension scores should be plotted to get the level of performance.

Note: It is important that the teacher train himself to listen carefully and record accurately errors made by the student. Practice will help to develop this skill. One should not expect to be an expert after the first administration.

FINDING THE READING LEVELS

Frustration Level

The student performing at the frustration level reads with symptoms such as fingerpointing, tension, or hesitant word-by-word reading. His comprehension may be extremely low. He is completely unable to handle the reading materials presented.

Instructional Level

At the instructional level, the student will be able to read with at least 93% accuracy of word recognition and with 75% or better comprehension. At this point, the teacher's help is necessary; but, after being given the instruction, the student should be able to handle the material independently.

Independent Level

At the independent level the student reads with ease. It is the level to be used in selecting supplementary reading material and library books. This means that the child has at least 97% word recognition and 90% comprehension.

Summary

1. Independent level: 97% and above correct oral reading and 90% and above comprehension
2. Instructional level: 93–96% oral reading and 75% and above comprehension
3. Frustration level: Below 93% oral reading and below 75% comprehension.

SILENT READING COMPREHENSION

Many teachers will find it unnecessary to give a silent comprehension test because it is too time consuming. However, for diagnostic purposes, it may be helpful to know the discrepancy between the child's oral and silent reading.

If a silent reading test is given, then the teacher may want to average the scores between the oral comprehension and the silent reading comprehension in order to get a more approximate grade level.

LISTENING COMPREHENSION LEVEL (OPTIONAL)

The teacher can read more difficult selections to the student after he has failed one to determine whether or not he can understand higher level material and discuss what he has heard. This is done beyond his instructional level. The highest level at which he can understand 75% of the material would determine his probable level of comprehension. Many professionals believe a student should be reading at this level of understanding. The listening comprehension scores can be recorded on the Developmental Reading Summary Record.

CHAP. 3   Developmental Reading Inventories

READING ERRORS TO LOOK FOR

Reading Errors Primarily Due to Auditory Channel Deficits

1. The student may mispronounce words, for example, read the word "chimney" as "chimley" (auditory acuity and/or discrimination).
2. He may take wild guesses where there is no relationship between the word seen and the word read (auditory–visual associative memory).
3. When stuck on a word, the student may not be able to "sound it out" (auditory–visual associative memory).
4. He may be poor in blending sounds together to make words (auditory closure).
5. He may use a synonym, for example, saying "mommy" for "mother" (auditory–visual associative memory).
6. He may substitute words, such as saying "a" for "the" (auditory–visual associative memory).

Reading Errors Primarily Due to Visual Channel Deficits

1. The student may exhibit word-by-word reading or poor phrasing (rate of perception).
2. He may be unable to keep his place and may skip lines or parts of lines when reading (visual figure-ground or ocular motor).
3. He may add words which may or may not change the meaning, for example, adding the word "the" when it isn't there (visual memory and/or misperception).
4. He may repeat parts of words, phrases, and sometimes whole sentences in an attempt to get the meaning (check receptive and expressive language).
5. He may read through punctuation distorting the meaning of what he reads (check receptive and expressive language).
6. He may reverse words or letters (visual sequential memory and/or spatial).
7. He may invert words or letters (visual—memory and/or spatial).
8. He may look at the beginning of a word and then say some other word that starts in the same way, for example, "surprise" for "something." If he self-corrects, he may be only looking at initial consonants and configurations (rate of perception)

MANN-SUITER DEVELOPMENTAL READING SUMMARY RECORD

The examiner should plot the scores for each area of reading on the Developmental Reading Summary Record (Figure 3.6) to determine the child's present level of functioning. The procedure for plotting the scores is as follows:
1. Record the percentage word-recognition, correct flash scores in the appropriate boxes. These scores are used for diagnostic purposes only, giving information as to how quickly and how accurately a student perceives a word.

FIGURE 3.6 Mann-Suiter Developmental Reading Summary Record

NAME _____ GRADE _____ AGE _____ DATE _____
EXAMINER _____
DEVELOPMENTAL WORD RECOGNITION AND READING INVENTORY

		pp3	P	1	2^1	2^2	3^1	3^2	4	5	6
1	% Word recognition, correct-flash										
2	% Word recognition, correct-untimed (ut)										
3	% Word recognition, accuracy-(DPRI) oral reading										
4	% Word recognition, average — UT and DPRI oral reading (2 and 3)*										
5	% Reading comprehension, form ___										
6	% Listening comprehension, form ___										

Average of the Untimed Word Recognition and the DPRI Oral Reading.

*Difficulties noted:

Reading Comprehension (y-axis: 100, 95, 90, 85, 80, 75, 70, 65, 60, 55, 50, 45) vs % (x-axis: 100, 99, 98, 97, 96, 95, 94, 93, 92, 91, 90, 89, 88, 87, 86)

INDEPENDENT / INSTRUCTIONAL / FRUSTRATION

Frustration Level _____
Instructional Level _____
Independent Level _____

41

CHAP. 3   Developmental Reading Inventories

2. Record the percentage word-recognition, correct-untimed scores and the percentage word-recognition accuracy from the paragraph oral readings in the appropriate boxes. These two scores are averaged to give the percentage word-recognition average and are recorded in the appropriate boxes.
3. Record the reading comprehension and note the appropriate form. Then record the listening comprehension score if given.
4. Plot the final scores on the graph indicating the level of functioning such as PP3 or P, etc., in the appropriate section — independent, instructional, or frustration.

MANN-SUITER DEVELOPMENTAL PARAGRAPH READING INVENTORY (FORM A)

The following inventory provides examples of means to determine the reading levels of students. The teacher should follow instructions beginning on p. 34.

(Note: Primer type is recommended in reproducing the student copies for primer through level one selections.)

MANN-SUITER DEVELOPMENTAL PARAGRAPH READING INVENTORY
(TEACHER SCORING SHEET)

MOTIVATIONAL QUESTION: Have you ever seen a red dog? Find out what kind of a dog Jane and Dick saw in this story.

Pre-Primer 3   (29 words — Form A)

THE RED DOG

"Look, look," said Jane.

"See the funny little dog.

Can you see it?

It is red."

"I see it," said Dick.

"It is a toy dog."

Errors:	0	1	2	3	4	5
	100	97	93	89	86	83

Detail	1.	What did Jane see? (a funny little dog, a red dog, or a toy dog)
Vocabulary		What is the meaning of the word "little"? (small, etc.)
Main Idea	2.	Why did Jane call the little dog funny? (it was red)
Inference	3.	Where do you think the children were? (toy store, etc.)
Detail	4.	What kind of a dog did Dick say it was? (toy) ✓

Errors:	0	1	2	3
	100	75	50	25

MANN-SUITER DEVELOPMENTAL PARAGRAPH READING INVENTORY
(TEACHER SCORING SHEET)

MOTIVATIONAL QUESTION: Have you seen a baby animal? This story is about a cute baby animal that a little girl named Ann saw.

Primer   (40 words — Form A)

THE BABY MONKEY

One day Ann went

for a walk in the zoo.

Soon she saw something.

"A baby monkey," said Ann.

"I see a baby monkey."

Then she saw Mary and Jimmy.

"Come see the baby monkey," called Ann.

Errors: 0   1   2   3   4   5   6
         100   98   95   93   90   88   85

Detail	1.	Where was Ann walking? (in the zoo)
Main Idea	2.	Why was Ann excited? (she saw a baby monkey)
Detail	3.	How many children are in the story? (three)
Vocabulary		What is the meaning of the word "zoo"? (any acceptable answer)
Inference	4.	Why do you think Ann wanted Mary and Jimmy to see the baby monkey? (any acceptable answer)

Errors: 0   1   2   3
         100   75   50   25

MANN-SUITER DEVELOPMENTAL PARAGRAPH READING INVENTORY
(TEACHER SCORING SHEET)

MOTIVATIONAL QUESTION: The family in this story went to a park. Read to find out what mother forgot to take with her.

First Reader   (51 words — Form A)

FUN AT THE PARK

One hot day we went to a park to swim.

Other people were at the park, too.

"Let's get a hot dog on a bun," said Dick.

"I want ice cream," said Lisa.

"O-o-o-!" Mother cried.

"I left my money at home."

"I have some," said Dick.

Errors:	0	1	2	3	4	5	6	7
	100	98	96	94	92	90	88	86

Detail	1.	What kind of a day was it? (hot)
Inference	2.	What time of day do you think it was? (afternoon, around noon, lunch time)
Main Idea	3.	What were the children planning to do at the park? (have fun, eat hot dogs, swim)
Inference	4.	How do you think Lisa felt when Mother said she forgot her money? (upset, sad, angry)
Vocabulary		What is the meaning of the words "hot dog"? (weiner, frankfurter, etc.)

Errors:	0	1	2	3
	100	75	50	25

MANN-SUITER DEVELOPMENTAL PARAGRAPH READING INVENTORY
(TEACHER SCORING SHEET)

MOTIVATIONAL QUESTION: Have you ever earned your own money? The children in this story wanted some money. Let's see how they decide to earn it.

2¹Reader   (55 words — Form A)

THE LEMONADE STAND

It was a hot summer day.

Bill and Ann wished they could make some money.

Ann said, "Why don't we have a lemonade stand?"

"I know where we can get some ice and lemons to make lemonade," said Bill.

"I'll ask John to help us," said Ann.

"He can get the ice."

Errors:	0	1	2	3	4	5	6	7
	100	98	96	94	93	91	89	87

Vocabulary — What is the meaning of the words "lemonade stand"? (any acceptable response)

Main Idea   1. Why did the children decide to have a lemonade stand? (to earn money)
Detail   2. What kind of a day was it? (hot summer day)
Detail   3. What did the children say they were going to get to make lemonade? (ice and lemons)
Inference   4. What other things do you think they will need in order to make lemonade? (water and sugar)

Errors:	0	1	2	3
	100	75	50	25

MANN-SUITER DEVELOPMENTAL PARAGRAPH READING INVENTORY
(TEACHER SCORING SHEET)

MOTIVATIONAL QUESTION: Have you ever looked at the stars at night? What do they look like to you? This story is about a boy and girl who saw something different in the sky one night.

2^2 Reader   (61 words — Form A)

A VISITOR FROM OUTER SPACE

One night Ann and Bill were looking at stars.

"Look Ann," said Bill, "Something flashed across the sky."

"I saw it too," said Ann.

"It must have been a shooting star."

"Where do shooting stars come from?" asked Bill.

"I don't know," said Ann.

"Let's ask father."

Father said, "They are burning rocks from outer space."

Errors:	0	1	2	3	4	5	6	7	8
	100	98	97	95	93	91	90	88	87

Detail	1.	What were the children doing? (looking at stars)
Inference	2.	What time of day was it? (night)
Main Idea	3.	Why is this story called, "A visitor from outer space?" (the visitor is the shooting star and it's from outer space)
Detail	4.	What did father say shooting stars were? (burning rocks)
Detail	5.	Where do shooting stars come from? (outer space)
Vocabulary		What is another word for shooting star? (meteorite, falling star, etc.)

Errors:	0	1	2	3
	100	80	60	40

MANN-SUITER DEVELOPMENTAL PARAGRAPH READING INVENTORY
(TEACHER SCORING SHEET)

MOTIVATIONAL QUESTION: Have you ever seen a big fire? This story tells about a very large fire and what a little girl thought would put it out.

3^1 Reader   (70 words — Form A)

THE FIRE IN THE EVERGLADES

"There are many fires in the Everglades National Park," said the TV announcer.

"The fires are spreading to the Indian villages.

Smoke is clouding the sky.

The animals are being forced to leave their homes."

Ann thought, "If we only had some rain, then the animals would not have to run away.

I hope that it rains soon so the fires will be put out."

Errors:	0	1	2	3	4	5	6	7	8
	100	98	97	96	95	93	92	90	89

Vocabulary		What is the meaning of the word "announcer"? (a person who announces information on the radio or TV)
Detail	1.	How did Ann find out about the fires? (TV announcer)
Detail	2.	What was clouding the sky? (Smoke)
Main Idea	3.	Why was everyone worried about the fire? (it was spreading, animals could get hurt, Indians endangered, etc.)
Detail	4.	Where was the fire? (Everglades National Park)

Errors:	0	1	2	3	4
	100	80	60	40	20

(Note: Everglades National Park is a proper name and therefore not counted as an error.)

48

MANN-SUITER DEVELOPMENTAL PARAGRAPH READING INVENTORY
(TEACHER SCORING SHEET)

MOTIVATIONAL QUESTION: Would you go swimming if you were told not to? This is a story about a boy who disobeyed his mother and found himself in trouble.

3^2 Reader   (96 words — Form A)

SWIMMING ALONE

It was a dark and cloudy day but Bill went swimming alone in the rough water.

His mother had told him not to go because it was such a poor day for swimming.

Bill disobeyed her and went away.

He soon swam out over his head and realized in a panic that he could not get back to the shore.

Luckily, there was a woman on the beach who heard his screams for help.

A boat soon came to his rescue.

Bill did not disobey his mother again by swimming alone in rough water.

Errors:	0	1	2	3	4	5	6	7	8	9	10
	100	99	98	97	96	95	94	93	92	90	89

Vocabulary		What is the meaning of the word disobeyed? (to refuse, or to fail to obey)
Detail	1.	What kind of a day was it? (dark and cloudy)
Detail	2.	Who went swimming with Bill? (no one)
Main Idea	3.	Why did Bill's mother tell him not to go swimming? (because it was such a poor day, rough water, dark and cloudy day)
Detail	4.	How was he rescued? (a boat)
Inference	5.	How do you think Bill feels now about swimming alone in rough water? (any logical answer)

Errors:	0	1	2	3	4
	100	80	60	40	20

MANN-SUITER DEVELOPMENTAL PARAGRAPH READING INVENTORY
(TEACHER SCORING SHEET)

MOTIVATIONAL QUESTION: This story is about a dog who went to the movies.

4 Reader   (124 words — Form A)

DUKE GOES TO THE MOVIES

Duke and his master went to the movies.

The manager said, "You can't take a dog in there.

It's against the rules."

"This is no ordinary dog," said Duke's master.

"He is well behaved and has a collar.

If he becomes noisy, we will leave."

After the show, the manager spoke to Duke's master.

He said that he was watching Duke and noticed that the dog wagged his tail

for the happy parts of the movie.

He yawned when it became dull and whined a little at the sad parts.

"What an amazing dog!" said the manager.

"Did he enjoy the movie?"

Duke's master said, "I think he may have been a little bored since he read the book."

Errors:	0	1	2	3	4	5	6	7	8	9	10	11	12
	100	99	98	98	97	96	95	94	93	92	91	91	90

Vocabulary		What is the meaning of the word "master" in this story? (his owner)
Detail	1.	Who didn't want to let Duke into the movies? (the manager)
Detail	2.	Why aren't dogs allowed in the movies? (against the rules)
Main Idea	3.	What made Duke an unusual dog? (wagged tail for happy parts, yawned when dull, whined when sad, read the book)
Inference	4.	Do you think the other people in the theatre were upset with Duke? (no — Duke made no loud noise)
Detail	5.	What did Duke do when he became bored? (yawned)

Errors:	0	1	2	3	4
	100	80	60	40	20

MANN-SUITER DEVELOPMENTAL PARAGRAPH READING INVENTORY (TEACHER SCORING SHEET)

MOTIVATIONAL QUESTION: Have you ever dusted furniture? Some people don't want their's dusted. See what Mr. Bradshaw's reasons are for not dusting his furniture.

5 Reader   (93 words — Form A)

LEAVE THE DUST ALONE

Mr. Bradshaw had an antique shop in a small New England town.

The dust was so thick you could hardly find your way around.

He used to repair old furniture and sell it to people from the big cities who came wandering through his little shop.

People would ask, "How much for this beat-up old chair with the dust on it?"

They thought it was old and they had a bargain.

Many liked to rummage through the dust.

"The dustier the better," he would say to his wife.

Errors:	0	1	2	3	4	5	6	7	8	9	10
	100	99	98	97	96	94	93	92	91	90	89

Vocabulary		What is the meaning of the word "rummage"? (to search through things)
Detail	1.	What kind of a shop did Mr. Bradshaw own? (antique shop)
Detail	2.	Where was the shop located? (small New England town)
Main Idea	3.	Why didn't Mr. Bradshaw want to dust his furniture? (wanted it to look old)
Inference	4.	Why do you think people liked the dusty old furniture? (they thought it was old and they had a bargain)
Detail	5.	Where did people come from who bought his furniture? (big cities)

Errors:	0	1	2	3	4
	100	80	60	40	20

MANN-SUITER DEVELOPMENTAL PARAGRAPH READING INVENTORY
(TEACHER SCORING SHEET)

MOTIVATIONAL QUESTION: Have your friends ever teased you? Here's a story about someone who was teased and what he did about it.

6 Reader   (138 words — Form A)

A SENSE OF HUMOR

Rosemary walked John to his classroom every day.

She was ten and he was only seven.

John was blind and when he got off the bus, he needed someone to escort

him to his room.

Rosemary was crippled, but her handicap did not prevent her from traveling

to school alone.

"What color is my blouse?" she queried one day.

"I don't know," exclaimed John.

"You can't see it," she retorted.

"It's lavender. What color is the ribbon in my hair?"

"I don't know," sighed John.

"It's crimson," she giggled.

"but you can't see it."

It was obvious that John was being teased, but he didn't lose his patience.

After thinking for a while, he said quite seriously,

"Rosemary, what color is my underwear? You don't know, do you?

That's because you can't see it."

Errors:	0	1	2	3	4	5	6	7	8	9	10	11
	100	99	98	97	97	96	95	94	94	93	92	91

Detail	1.	Why did John need someone to walk him to class? (he was blind)
Detail	2.	How did John get to school? (bus)
Inference	3.	Do you think Rosemary was mean? (any rational answer)
Inference	4.	How do we know that John was being teased? (Rosemary's questions)
Main Idea	5.	What did John use to solve a situation that could have been serious? (An answer that infers humor or intelligence)
Vocabulary		What does the word "obvious" mean? (evident, apparent, clear)

Errors:	0	1	2	3	4
	100	80	60	40	20

CHAPTER 4

SUPPLEMENTARY EVALUATION AND SPECIAL FORMS

The supplementary evaluation section is designed to provide the teacher and others who are concerned with diagnosing the problems of learning handicapped children with a list of commonly used tests related to the various areas of learning. Individuals involved with assessment may wish to reinforce their findings by utilizing standardized tests which measure different learning characteristics in children. Professionals from other disciplines may already be using as a part of their basic testing battery several of these instruments. It is important that individuals who become responsible for defining and interpreting test data and communicating this information to teachers in a meaningful way, be able to relate this data directly to the findings attained through informal or developmental evaluation compiled by the teacher. Psychologists and special resource teachers who may be more knowledgeable and sophisticated in the area of evaluation working together with regular classroom teachers present a more comprehensive approach to defining particular learning problems in children. The classroom teacher should become informed as to what these particular tests measure. This does not mean that expertise is required in all areas of evaluation but that the classroom teacher should at least have some basic understanding of the assessment devices presently being used in different educational settings. Each of the evaluation instruments indicated has bibliographic information listed in the appropriate section of the handbook.

GENERAL READINESS

1. Boehm Test of Basic Concepts. (Boehm 1970)
2. Anton Brenner Developmental Test of School Readiness. (Boston University 1955)
3. Clymer-Barrett Prereading Battery. (Clymer and Barrett 1969)

CHAP. 4   Supplementary Evaluation and Special Forms

4. Evanston Early Identification Scale. (Landsman and Dillard 1967)
5. First Grade Screening Test. (Pate and Webb 1966)
6. Gesell Developmental Test. (Ilg and Ames 1965, Behavior Tests)
7. Meeting Street School Screening Test. (Hamsworth and Siqueland 1969)
8. Metropolitan Readiness Test. (Hildreth and Griffiths 1966)
9. Screening Test of Academic Readiness. (Ahr 1966)
10. Valett Developmental Survey of Basic Learning (Valett 1967, Valett Developmental Survey)
11. Vane Kindergarten test. (Vane 1968)

AUDITORY MODALITY

Acuity

1. Audiometric Sweep Test.

Perception

DISCRIMINATION

1. Boston University Speech Sound Discrimination Test. (Boston University 1955)
2. Goldman-Fristoe-Woodcock Test of Auditory Discrimination. (Goldman, Friscoe, and Woodcock 1970)
3. PERC Auditory Discrimination Test. (Drake 1965)
4. Wepman Test of Auditory Discrimination. (Wepman 1958)

CLOSURE

1. Auditory Closure Subtest of the Illinois Test of Psycholinguistic Abilities. (Kirk, McCarthy, and Kirk 1968)
2. Roswell-Chall Auditory Blending Test. (Roswell and Chall 1963)

Imagery (Memory-Sequencing)

1. Detroit Test of Learning Aptitude Subtests 6 and 13. (Baker and Leland 1959)
2. Digit Span subtest of the Wechsler Intelligence Scale for Children (WISC). (Wechsler 1955)
3. Memory Subtest of the Illinois Test of Psycholinguistic Abilities. (Kirk, McCarthy, and Kirk 1968)
4. Strauss and Lehtinen Ability to Produce Tapped Out Patterns (Strauss and Lehtinen 1947).
5. Sentences Subtest of the Wechsler Pre-school and Primary Scale of Intelligence (WPPSI). (Wechsler 1967)

VISUAL MODALITY

Acuity and Ocular Motor

1. Keystone Visual Survey Telebinocular. (Keystone View Co. 1958)
2. Snellen Chart. (American Medical Association)
3. Spache Binocular Vision Test (Keystone View Co. 1961)
4. Ortho-rater (Bausch and Lomb 1958)

Perception

DISCRIMINATION

1. Marianne Frostig Developmental Test of Visual Perception. (Frostig 1963)
2. Marion Monroe Visual Test #1 (Ilg and Ames 1965 *School Readiness*)
3. Metropolitan Readiness Test. (Hildreth, Griffiths, and McGauvran 1966)

CLOSURE

1. Illinois Test of Psycholinguistic Abilities Visual Closure Subtest. (Kirk, McCarthy, and Kirk 1968)

FIGURE-GROUND

1. Marianne Frostig Developmental Test of Visual Perception. (Frostig 1963)
2. Strauss and Lehtinen Figure Background Cards. (Strauss and Lehtinen 1947)

Imagery (Memory-sequencing)

1. Benton Visual Retention Test. (Benton 1963)
2. Detroit Test of Learning Aptitude Subtests 9 and 16. (Baker and Leland 1959)
3. Graham-Kendall Memory for Designs Test. (Graham and Kendall 1960)
4. Marion Monroe Test #3 (Ilg and Ames 1965 *School Readiness*)

Visual-motor (Gross and Fine)

1. Beery Developmental Test of Visual-Motor Integration (Beery 1967)
2. Bender Visual-Motor Gestalt Test. (Bender 1938; Koppitz 1964)
3. Detroit Test of Learning Aptitude, Subtest #5. (Baker and Leland 1959)

CHAP. 4   Supplementary Evaluation and Special Forms

4. Goodenough-Harris Draw-A-Man Test. (Goodenough 1926)
5. Harris Test of Lateral Dominance. (Harris 1958)
6. Marianne Frostig Developmental Test of Visual Perception. (Frostig 1963)
7. Minnesota Percepto-Diagnostic Test. (Fuller and Laird 1963)
8. Purdue Perceptual Motor Survey (Kephart and Roach 1966)
9. Standardized Road Map Test of Direction Sense. (Money, Alexander, and Walker 1965)
10. Winter Haven Designs (Winter Haven Lions Club 1956)

LANGUAGE

1. Houston Test of Language Development. (Houston Press 1963)
2. Illinois Test of Psycholinguistic Abilities. (Kirk, McCarthy, and Kirk 1968)
3. Peabody Picture Vocabulary Test. (Dunn 1959)
4. Picture Story Language Test. (Pronovost and Dumbleton 1953)
5. Slingerland Screening Tests for Specific Language Disabilities. (Slingerland 1964)
6. Verbal Language Development Scale. (Mecham 1959)

Speech Tests

1. Deep Test of Articulation. (McDonald 1964)
2. Templin Darley Tests of Articulation. (Templin and Darley 1960)

SOCIAL-EMOTIONAL

1. Bender Gestalt Test for Young Children. (Bender 1938; Koppitz 1964)
2. Children's Apperception Test (CAT). (Bellak and Bellak 1949–55)
3. Goodenough-Harris Draw-A-Man Test. (Goodenough 1926)
4. House-Tree-Person (HTP). (Bieliauskas 1963)
5. Thematic Apperception Test (TAT). (Bellak 1954)

MANN-SUITER ANALYSIS OF ERRORS SHEET

After having given the Developmental Inventories, it is suggested that the teacher then indicate the errors on the Analysis of Errors Sheet to follow. Having done this, the teacher will then be better able to determine how much and what type of additional testing is necessary prior to formulating any educational strategies for a given student. Some teachers will require more information to include standardized tests before making any decisions. The question is not how much testing is adequate but, rather, how much information is needed in order to make a decision about changing or modifying the educational program for a particular student.

MANN-SUITER DEVELOPMENTAL INVENTORIES

Analysis of Errors (Language Arts)

Name _____ School _____

Date _____ Grade _____ Date of Birth _____

Examiner _____

DEVELOPMENTAL SPELLING INVENTORY

(A check mark indicates difficulty)

Auditory Errors

1. Substitutions (*t* for *d*, *f* for *v*, *sh* for *ch*) ____
2. Omits vowels (*brd* for *bird*) ____
3. Omits second consonant in blends (*rut* for *rust*) ____
4. Uses synonyms (*house* for *home*) ____
5. Wild guessing (*yot* for *yes*) ____
6. No response ____
7. Vowel sound confusion (*but* for *bat*) ____
8. Omits word endings such as *ed*, *s*, *ing* ____
9. Cannot remember spelling rules ____

Visual Errors

1. Writes the beginning letters only ____
2. Reversals of words or letters (*b* for *d*, or *on* for *no*) ____
3. Inversions of letters (*m* for *w*) ____
4. Mixture of capital and small letters (*baBy*) ____
5. Spells phonetically (cannot revisualize) ____

Other Errors

CHAP. 4   Supplementary Evaluation and Special Forms

DEVELOPMENTAL WORD READING INVENTORY (A check mark indicates difficulty)

Auditory Errors

1. Complete guess ___
2. Knows letter names, but not sounds ___
3. Associative error (*house* for *home*) ___
4. Knows sounds but cannot blend into words ___
5. Substitutes one sound for another ___

Visual Errors

1. Slow rate of perception (fails flash, but gets untimed) ___
2. Sees beginning of word only or beginning and endings only on flash ___
3. Reversals (*was* for *saw*) ___
4. Inversions (*me* for *we*) ___
5. Does not discriminate fine detail (*ship* for *snip*) ___
6. Omits sounds from words (check auditory discrimination) ___
7. Adds sounds ___
8. Hesitations ___

Other Errors

DEVELOPMENTAL PARAGRAPH READING INVENTORY

Auditory Errors

1. Mispronunciation (*forgē* for *forge*, etc.) ___
2. Wild guess ___
3. Associative errors: (*house* for *home*) ___

Developmental Paragraph Reading Inventory

4. Knows sounds but cannot blend
5. Words pronounced for child
6. Substitutions (*a* for *the*)
7. Cannot sound the word out

Visual Errors

1. Reversals of words (*was* for *saw*)
2. Transposition of words and phrases (*said John* for *John said*)
3. Inversions (*me* for *we*)
4. Repetitions
5. Loses place and skips lines
6. Omits words or word endings
7. Errors of visual discrimination (reads *ship* for *snip*, or *ear* for *car*)
8. Word by word
9. Reads through punctuation.
10. Hesitations.
11. Addition of words and/or endings

Other Errors

Comprehension

READING LEVEL
1. Detail
2. Main Idea
3. Inference
4. Vocabulary
   a. Primarily Concrete-Functional (C–F)
   b. Primarily abstract (A)

59

CHAP. 4   Supplementary Evaluation and Special Forms

General Observations on Oral Reading

1. Phrasing
2. Fluency
3. Finger pointing

General Observations on Silent Reading

1. Uses fingers
2. Vocalizes
3. Makes remarks

Listening Comprehension

1. Grade level expectancy based on listening comprehension

Handwriting Errors

1. Unable to copy accurately
2. Poor alignment of letters
3. Unorthodox joining of letters in cursive
4. Fusion of letters
5. Changes hands
6. Writes from right to left
7. Fatigues easily
8. Poor letter formation
9. Irregular size letters
10. Poor spacing

Other Errors

DEVELOPMENTAL SCREENING

(A check mark indicates difficulty)

Visual

1. Visual Motor   ____
2. Visual Discrimination ____
3. Visual Memory   ____
4. Visual Closure   ____

Auditory

1. Auditory Discrimination   ____
2. Auditory Closure   ____
3. Auditory Memory (sentences)   ____
4. Alphabet-Speech Screen (auditory-visual association)

Language

1. Visual Language Classification   ____
2. Visual Language Association   ____
3. Auditory Language Classification ____
4. Auditory Language Association   ____
5. Manual Language Expression   ____
6. Speech   ____
7. Verbal Language Expression   ____
8. Written Language Expression   ____
9. Non-verbal Language   ____

MANN-SUITER DIAGNOSTIC WORKSHEET

After having completed the Analysis of Errors Sheet, and then having given any additional tests which tend to either support or negate the findings of the Developmental Inventories, the teacher is ready to summarize the results. The Diagnostic Worksheet can then be used to summarize all information gained through both formal and informal evaluations. This will further aid the teacher in terms of formulating educational strategies for a particular student.

CHAP. 4   Supplementary Evaluation and Special Forms

MANN-SUITER DIAGNOSTIC WORKSHEET

Strengths   Average   Weaknesses

Auditory

SENSORY (Acuity)
PERCEPTION:
Figure-ground
Closure
Discrimination
Localization-attention

IMAGERY:
Memory
Auditory-Auditory association
Auditory-Visual Association
Sequencing

Visual

SENSORY (Acuity)
PERCEPTION:
Figure-ground
Closure
Discrimination

IMAGERY:
Memory
Sequencing

Strengths   Average   Weaknesses

Language

Visual Language Classification
Visual Language Association
Auditory Language Classification
Auditory Language Association
Manual Language Expression

62

Mann-Suiter Diagnostic Worksheet

Alphabet Speech Screen (letter names and sounds)
Verbal Language Expression
Written Language Expression
Non-verbal Symbolic Language

Conceptualization

Vocabulary essentially concrete–functional
Vocabulary essentially abstract

Listening Comprehension

Level at which student understands 50% or more of paragraphs read to him

Motor

Fine motor (handwriting)
Gross motor

Spelling

Reading

Arithmetic

Speech

Articulation
Stuttering
Voice

Comments:

MANN-SUITER EDUCATIONAL PROFILE

Green ✓ = strong
Red ✓ = weak
Black x = average
Unmarked = not tested

Name _____
Date of Birth _____
Date _____
Grade _____

Examiner _____

Address _____
School _____
Teacher _____
Student's Home Phone _____

Auditory

Sensory
Acuity ☐

Perception
Discrimination ☐ ☐
Localization and attention
Figure-ground ☐ ☐
Closure

Imagery
Memory ☐ ☐
Auditory–auditory association ☐
Auditory–visual association
Sequencing ☐

Visual

Sensory
Acuity ☐
Fusion ☐
Convergence ☐

Perception
Discrimination ☐
Figure-ground ☐ ☐
Closure

Imagery
Memory ☐ ☐
Sequencing

Motor

Fine ☐ ☐ ☐ ☐
Gross
Spatial
Left–right orientation
Body image ☐

Academic Tasks

Reading

Comprehension and Concept level (Concrete–Functional, C–F, or Abstract A)

Writing (Handwriting and Expression)

Spelling

Arithmetic

Language

Receptive
Visual language classification ☐ ☐ ☐ ☐
Visual language association
Auditory language classification
Auditory language association ☐
Expressive
Manual language expression ☐ ☐ ☐
Speech
Verbal language expression
Written language expression
Non-verbal language

Other

Controls

Distractability ☐
Perseveration ☐
Disinhibition ☐
Hyperactivity ☐
Overstimulation ☐
Inhibiting responses ☐
Understimulation ☐

MANN-SUITER EDUCATIONAL PROFILE

After completing the Diagnostic Worksheet, the teacher can then indicate the strengths and weaknesses of a particular student by checking the various areas on the Educational Profile with the appropriate colored pencils and also write in the recommended task-level opions. This concise report can also be used to describe the needs of a student to other school personnel. It should become a part of the student's cumulative record and be sent along with him should he be transferred to another school.

CHAPTER 5

DEFICIT LEVEL CURRICULUM (PROCESS ORIENTED)

The instructor will find the following deficit areas of learning as delineated with accompanying educational activities helpful in planning a specific program for a student exhibiting one or more difficulties in the processing of information.

Students exhibiting learning problems may be impeded in the following manner: (1) *intra-channel disorders* whereby the student may have difficulty in processing information that can be said to be more visual or more auditory in nature, for example, being unable to discriminate symbols (*a* from *o*) or sounds ("f" from "v") one from the other at the level of perception; and (2) *inter-channel disorders* whereby the student may have difficulty using auditory and visual clues simultaneously, for example, he may recognize the letter but be unable to recall the sound, or he may understand what is required of him (auditory association) but be unable to respond to terms of a motor act (expression).

This section will deal with deficit analysis to include observable behaviors and educational activities in the following process areas:

1. Auditory channel
2. Visual channel
3. Motor
4. Language
5. Control factors
6. Motivational and emotional factors.

CHAP. 5   Deficit Level Curriculum

AUDITORY CHANNEL

Deficits in the Auditory Sensory Area

AUDITORY ACUITY. Difficulty in hearing may come about as a result of the following physical disorders:

1. *The vibrator or sound producer* — loss of specific frequencies may prevent the student from hearing certain sounds and teachers who have either low or high pitched voices.
2. *The acoustic signal or sound in the air* — a clogged up ear canal will affect the ability to hear. Some young children are continually putting things into their ears. This must be checked by the teacher. Excessive build up of wax may also affect hearing.
3. *The mechanical signal or eardrum and/or bones of the middle ear* — damage to the eardrum itself or to the bones of the middle ear can result in mild to severe hearing loss and require the use of a hearing aid.
4. *The hydraulic signal or the inner-ear fluid* — inner-ear infection can cause difficulty in hearing.
5. *The electrical signal or the Cochlea Nerve* — damage to the cochlea nerve may result in moderate to profound hearing loss and is quite difficult to treat.

Observable Behaviors:

1. The child may cup his ear to hear.
2. He may be restless and exhibit poor behavior.
3. He may have difficulty following directions.
4. He may consistently ask for repetitions.
5. He may turn his head unusually when he tries to listen.

Educational Activities:

1. The student should be referred for an auditory examination.
2. His seat should be changed so he will be closer to the source of sound. The teacher should avoid seating the student near noisy air conditioners, windows, or doors.
3. The teacher should face the child when giving directions. Many teachers talk to the chalkboard.
4. Amplification would be helpful.
5. The teacher should not speak from behind the student.
6. The teacher should watch his rate and amount of speech or verbal input.

Auditory Channel

Deficits in Auditory Perception

PROBLEMS WITH AUDITORY ATTENTION TO SOUND

Observable Behaviors:

1. A student with this problem may be easily distracted by competing stimuli.
2. He may appear to be emotionally disturbed or mentally retarded.
3. Some children have difficulty getting meaning from sound or speech and, therefore, do not attend to auditory stimuli.

Educational Activities:

1. The teacher should create an awareness of sound by amplifying.
2. He can attract the student's attention by using toys and musical instruments.
3. He can use a clicker or some other sound signal to get the attention of the student.
4. In severe cases, the teacher may have to turn the child's head to the source of the sound.

PROBLEMS WITH SOUND LOCALIZATION

Observable Behaviors:

1. The child may have difficulty finding the source of sound or the direction from which it is coming.
2. He may have difficulty in assigning specific voices to specific persons.
3. Some teachers have their desk in the back of the room and give directions from behind children. The student will need to find the teacher's voice before he can attend to any directions. The teacher should face the child when he is speaking to him.
4. To identify this problem, the teacher could perform a simple "snap test" — ask the student to close his eyes, then the teacher should snap his fingers around the student's body and have the student point to the direction of the sound. If he cannot point to where the sound is coming from, he may have problems with auditory localization.

Educational Activities:

1. The student should practice locating sounds of bells, noise makers, and then, voices around the room with sight and then blindfolded.
2. Outdoor activities can be applied as well whereby the child closes his eyes and tells the teacher what he hears and in which direction the sound is coming from.
3. Blindfolded, the student matches the person with the voice of fellow classmates.
4. The teacher can hide a sound making device such as a small radio for the student to find.
5. Parents can play sound finding games at home.

CHAP. 5   Deficit Level Curriculum

PROBLEMS WITH AUDITORY (SOUND) DISCRIMINATION

Observable Behaviors:

1. The child cannot tell when sounds are the same or different.
2. The student may have difficulty with pitch, frequency and intensity.
3. Some students have difficulty with distinguishing human vs. non-human sounds.
4. Similar sounding letters, i.e., *d/t* are often confused.
5. Problems may be evident with learning phonics and in blending sounds.

Educational Activities:

1. The teacher can begin with the recognition and discrimination of grossly different sounds in nature such as wind, rain, fire, thunder, etc.
2. Then the student should learn to discriminate social sounds such as horns, bells, birds, dogs, and other social noises.
3. Musical instruments can be utilized to teach recognition and discrimination of sounds.
4. Pure tones will help the child discriminate pitch, frequency, intensity, and timbre.
5. After teaching grossly different sounds, the teacher should move to finer and finer discriminations using tuning forks, musical instruments, and other sound making devices.
6. In teaching, he should not teach similar sounding letters for contrast, for example, he should not teach *p* and *b* or *f* and *v* together.
7. Most importantly, he should not overload in teaching. If he is going to teach sounds, he should teach them one at a time, never introducing more than one new sound in a given day.

PROBLEMS WITH AUDITORY FIGURE-GROUND

Observable Behaviors:

1. The student may exhibit forced attention to sound causing him to attend to extraneous noises in his environment.
2. He may find it difficult to attend to speech.
3. By comparison to other students, he may not be able to sit for long periods of time. He may appear to be distractable and hyperactive.
4. The teacher may find that the student obeys the commands of the teacher next door.
5. He may not be able to focus his attention on his own work and may tend to interfere when the teacher is working with another student.

Educational Activities:

1. The teacher should provide a place that is reasonably quiet where the student can get off by himself for parts of the day.
2. He should not seat the student by the window, door, or noisy air conditioner.
3. He can help him select relevant from irrelevant sounds in his environment with his eyes closed, then with his eyes open.

Auditory Channel

4. He can use tapes or records to help the student build in sound selectivity (ear phones can be used to screen out distraction).
5. Drugs under *strict supervision* may help.
6. The teacher should regulate the rate of input accordingly. Going slower makes a difference.
7. He can condition the student by introducing sound into the environment on a selective basis.

PROBLEMS WITH AUDITORY CLOSURE (BLENDING)

Observable Behaviors:

1. The student cannot blend sounds into syllables and words. Examples: He can read *c-a-t* in isolation but cannot put the sounds together to make the word *cat*.
2. He may not be able to put sounds together to make words that he hears orally.

Educational Activities:

1. The music teacher can provide activities that will aid the student in listening to the blending of tones.
2. The pushing together of anagrams, clay, and sandpaper letters will help the child "see" how sounds go together through physical blending.
3. Tapes of word analysis and synthesis, i.e., *cat—c at—c at—cat* are helpful. These can be put into games where he guesses the word from the sounds.
4. The teacher can use words based on the students' experiences.
5. In teaching reading, he should build on spelling patterns, i.e., at, am, an, op, et, etc., rather than on nonsense syllables.

Deficits in Auditory Imagery (Memory-Sequence)

The inability to remember what has been heard for both short and long periods is called *difficulty in reauditorization*. The student with this problem finds it difficult to recall what he has heard through the auditory modality.

Observable Behaviors:

1. The student may not be able to recall the sounds of things to include: (a) non-verbal sounds such as bells, animal sounds, horns, etc., and (b) verbal sounds such as letters, words, or sentences.
2. He may have difficulty in following a sequence of directions at home as well as in school.
3. He generally is able to understand and to recognize words but has difficulty retrieving them.
4. His parents may report that he never gets the phone message correct.
5. Memory deficits will also probably be observed by the physical education teacher, music teacher, etc.

CHAP. 5   Deficit Level Curriculum

Educational Activities:

For elementary grade students, the teacher can play "tell me games" to help the child with sequencing:

1. The teacher performs a series of auditory acts such as clap, stamp foot and close door with the student blindfolded and then asks "What did I do," "what did I do first," "next?," etc.
2. The child performs and the teacher says, "What did you do," etc.
3. Use sentence completion games, for example, "On the way to school, I saw a ____," and the next child repeats the sentence and adds one more thing, etc.
4. Singing songs, telling jokes, poems, and riddles are helpful.
5. The teacher can have the student listen to numerals and words and tell him how many he heard, then he can vary it by asking the student to repeat it in sequence.
6. For primary grade children, the teacher can place objects on a flannelboard and clap for each one.
7. Parents can play games such as "What did you hear first," "next," after visiting different places or by using noises in the home or neighborhood.
8. Parents should slow down the verbal input and reduce the number of directions given to the student.
9. The teacher can use chunking exercises, for example, telephone numbers, to practice the grouping and rhythm of long sequences.
10. He can use "echo games," for example, whisper a word, a phrase, or a sentence which then goes around the room.
11. He can have the students follow commands using an obstacle course.
12. He can use listening records and tapes.
13. He can use rhyming patterns.
14. He can play oral "Simple Simon" games with the students.
15. The teacher must slow down the rate of input accordingly.

VISUAL CHANNEL

Deficits in the Visual Sensory Area (Ocular-Motor Disorders)

DISTINGUISHING LIGHT FROM NO LIGHT.   The individual exhibits reduced sensitivity to light which is a prerequisite to efficient visual perception.

SEEING FINE DETAIL.   A student's disability in seeing fine detail can be determined through the Snellen Chart (American Medical Association), and a professional visual examination which measures visual acuity.

BINOCULAR FUSION.   The student may experience double vision resulting from uneven vision whereby the "bad eye" interferes with the "good eye." This can be diagnosed through the use of the (1) Telebinocular (Keystone View Co. 1958) (2) Ortho-rater (Bausch and Lomb 1958), or (3) Massachusetts Vision Test (Massachusetts Department of Public Health 1954).

CONVERGENCE. Convergence difficulties can be due to a muscular imbalance that interferes with the coordinated movement of the eyes resulting in the inability to focus properly. Ocular-motor activities under the direction of a professional in this area should be considered.

SCANNING. With scanning difficulties the child may not be able to perform (1) natural zig-zag scanning that may be required when he has to look at different things within the classroom, (2) visual pursuit or tracking of a moving object, or (3) the systematic learned eye movements that are required for reading.

Observable Behaviors:

1. Blinking
2. Crossed eyes
3. Clumsiness
4. Poor performance in physical education activities
5. Unusual head tilt in reading
6. Tearing, redness, or inflamation of eyes.

These symptoms may require medical attention and should be referred appropriately.

Deficits In Visual Perception (Recognition and Discrimination)

PROBLEMS WITH FIGURE-GROUND DIFFERENTIATION. The individual has difficulty in distinguishing an object from the irrelevant background and holding the image while scanning the total pattern.

Observable Behaviors:

1. The student may have difficulty in attending to the task assigned.
2. His written work may be disorganized.
3. He may form letters incorrectly when forced to write on a crowded page.
4. The student may have difficulty keeping his place while he reads or copies material.
5. He may skip sections of tests or omit parts in his workbook.
6. He may have difficulty in completing work presented on a crowded paper.
7. The most frequent complaint of the teacher is that he "never finishes his work."

CHAP. 5   Deficit Level Curriculum

Educational Activities:

1. The teacher can locate and describe objects for him in the street or playground.
2. He can locate and describe objects that are partially hidden in the classroom or home.
3. He can locate hidden objects and symbols in pictures to include geometric as well as other forms within the child's experience.
4. He can ask the student to listen and follow word-by-word book titles the teacher reads. The teacher holds up a book and reads the titles pointing to each word as he reads, then the student points as the teacher reads. The teacher should use simple titles at first to help the child differentiate the word from the space. The student does not need to be able to read the words.
5. The teacher should put the color into the materials and *not* overload the walls or the chalkboard with distracting color.
6. He should place pictures of geometric forms, objects, letters and words on newspaper for the student to locate and identify.
7. He should block out areas in workbooks so that the student would be able to attend better to specific tasks.

PROBLEMS WITH RECOGNITION AND DISCRIMINATION.   The student cannot discriminate differences and sameness as pertains to objects and symbols.

Observable Behaviors:

1. The student may know a word in context but not when presented in a new situation.
2. He may have difficulty in matching shapes, geometric forms, or symbols, i.e., letters, numerals, words, etc.
3. The child may have difficulty in recognizing people when they change a characteristic of their physical appearance.

Educational Activities:

1. *Concrete level* — The student should verbally describe the differences and similarities between objects. (*Note:* the student should be allowed to hold the objects as he describes them)
2. *Pictures* — (a) The teacher can use activity (ditto) sheets involving differences and similarities in pictures such as matching a smiling pumpkin with the one that looks different or the same. The learner should verbalize what is different or the same and how it is different or the same. (b) He can use photographs or pictures from magazines to aid the student in discriminating "difference" and "sameness" between objects and forms.
3. *Geometric Shapes* — (a) The teacher can use activities to include dittoes involving discrimination of geometric shapes. (b) He can ask the students to hole-match with geometric insets (this game is a good activity for younger children). (c) He can ask the students to find objects in the classroom or home that are of different size and shape.
4. *Letters and Words* — The teacher can develop activity sheets that facilitate the learning of differences and sameness in that order using letters, then words. A student could find the letter that looks like *m* or the word that looks like *ship*. Matching activities can be used here employing anagrams of felt, wooden or plastic letters.

Visual Channel

PROBLEMS WITH VISUAL CLOSURE. The student may have difficulty in visualizing a "whole" and omit portions or details from objects or symbols.

Observable Behaviors:

1. The student may have difficulty blending letters into words visually.
2. He may be able to read the word *cat* but if given the letters he cannot put them together to form the word.

Educational Activities:

1. The teacher should teach the blending of letters this way: [c] [at] and not this way [c] [a] [t] for students with this problem.
2. He can use activities involving the completion of simple to complex puzzles: 2 pieces, 3 pieces, 5 pieces, 9 pieces, etc.
3. Dot to dot pictures are helpful.
4. Completion of incomplete pictures is a good activity.
5. The teacher can use three dimensional puzzles.

PROBLEMS WITH OBJECT RECOGNITION (CENTRAL BLINDNESS)

Observable Behaviors:

1. The student may not be able to recognize objects but can see, describe, and reproduce objects. (This may be due to cerebral dysfunction.)
2. Sometimes the student may be able to recognize objects through touch.
3. He may have trouble integrating visual stimulus into a uniform whole and concentrates on the parts.

Educational Activities:

1. The teacher can utilize a card catalogue of words with associative pictures.
2. He can give the student a choice selection verbally: is it a ____, or ____, or ____.
3. Associating pictures or objects with sounds is a good activity.
4. The teacher can use concrete objects or pictures to associate with words.

Deficits in Visual Imagery (Memory-Sequencing)

The inability to remember what one has seen both for short and long periods of time is called difficulty with revisualization. The child with this process problem finds it difficult to recall what he has seen through the visual modality.

Observable Behaviors:

1. He may recognize the symbol when given a model but cannot recall it by himself.

CHAP. 5 Deficit Level Curriculum

2. He often experiences more difficulty in spelling and writing than in reading.
3. The student cannot "see" things or symbols in his mind's eye.
4. He may be able to remember all of the parts but he gets them in the wrong sequence (*hpoe* for *hope*).
5. He may be erratic or variable in the way he sequences words, spelling the word *the*, for example, *the*, hte, or teh; or he may have a fixed wrong image spelling the word *the* for example, teh consistently. The latter appears to be more difficult to ameliorate.

Educational Activities:

Basic to the amelioration process for children with memory problems is the concept that *recall must follow recognition*. In all activities, the child is asked to match first or to pick out one from among others before he is required to use his recall abilities.

1. *Reinforcing Visual Memory with Tactual–Kinesthetic Associations*—The student should be given an opportunity to establish a visual–tactual relationship by manipulating objects with his hands. The child with revisualization problems can be aided in his learning through the use of the tactual–kinesthetic modality. Touch and body awareness will make him more aware of differences and sameness at a more concrete level. The following sequence of activities will also be helpful to children who have difficulties in the area of visual perception as well as with visual memory.

Sequence in Teaching	*Visual–Tactual–Kinesthetic Associations*
Matching and comparing.	Matching a felt, wooden, plastic, clay, or sandpaper letter to another felt, wooden, plastic, clay, or sandpaper object or symbol (letter, word or numeral).
Tracing from a model.	The student traces over a felt, wooden, plastic, clay, or sandpaper object or symbol with his finger or walks or creeps over a pattern with his body.
Reproducing from a model. (Pencil, pen, clay, wet sand, finger paint, etc.)	The student copies from a felt, wooden, plastic, clay, or sandpaper model of an object or symbol (letter, word or numeral).
Reproducing without a model. (Pencil, pen, clay, wet sand, finger paint, etc.)	The student reproduces the object or symbol without the model present.

2. *Visual–Tactual Associations Using Shape as a Referent*
   a. Round and curved objects. The teacher should use spheres first and then any round object available to do the following:
      1) Let the learner take a suitably sized ball or sphere and cup it in his hands.
      2) Draw attention to the way it looks and feels, how it fits into the palms of his hands.
      3) Show him that he can turn it in any direction and feel its roundness.
      4) Call his attention to the fact that if his hands were large enough, they would fit around any ball and may even overlap.
      5) Using a ball, you could push a knitting needle through and show that if it pierces the center from any point on the surface, the distance is always the same.

Visual Channel

    b. Straight-edged objects. The teacher should start with a cube of wood or styrofoam shape to do the following:
        1) Have the learner put the shape into his hand to feel how it is unlike the sphere—it has straight edges and sharp corners which prick his palm.
        2) Let him feel along the straight lines and measure with his fingers or with a ruler to see that the edges are all the same length.
        3) Use rectangular solids and have the student discover differences by looking and feeling how these are not like cubes.
    c. Amelioration activities should include discrimination of shape, size, sequence, position, and color.

Note: The teacher should use concrete materials first if necessary, then pictures, geometric shapes, letters, and words. He should always proceed from that which is different to that which is the same.

3. *Activities Involving Auditory-Visual Associations*
    a. Listening and following directions. The teacher should ask the student to perform actions in certain sequences as in the following:
        1) Hopping, skipping, walking backwards, and forwards.
        2) Going in different directions to various places, turning around and touching objects with the left or right hand.
        3) Tapping with the left or right foot or hand a sequence of sounds.
    b. Visual Sequence and auditory associations.
        1. Rhythm of motion related to sound can be developed by skipping, walking, running, and tapping to music.
        2) The teacher can read sentences with rhymes, accenting the rhyming words, ask the student to repeat in the same way as he points to the words; for example: The *cat* and the *rat sat on a mat*.
        3) The teacher should say numerals in sequence emphasizing the even or odd ones as the student points to each one, for example,

                  <u>1</u> 2 <u>3</u> 4 <u>5</u> 6
                  1 <u>2</u> 3 <u>4</u> 5 <u>6</u>

and have the student repeat the same numbers that the teacher emphasized.
        4) The teacher should give the student plenty of practice in separating words into syllables so that he will hear and be able to repeat them in the proper order. This will help him with spelling as well as with pronunciation and will train him so that he will not be likely to make reversals or transpositions. For example, "draw" the syllables on the chalkboard, or on paper and have the student do the same. Have him say each syllable slowly as he does this. Start with two syllable words and go to longer ones. This activity is called "chunking" or "syllabication":

                        walk ing
                        small er
                        po si tion
                        fol low ing

Chunk numbers the same way; have the child look at them, cover them, and see if he can repeat them in groups forwards, then backwards. This gives practice in *sight-recall*.

CHAP. 5   Deficit Level Curriculum

MOTOR

Deficits in the Area of Body Image

The student may have difficulty in relating himself spatially to his environment. This can also be described as a lack of inner awareness of body as the physical parts of self relate to each other and to the physical environment.

Observable Behaviors:

1. The student may have difficulty in locating different parts of his body when asked to do so.
2. He may have difficulty in organizing himself to do a physical task such as moving furniture, etc.
3. He may exhibit a faulty body image as indicated by distortions in the Draw-A Person Test or in his human figure drawings. (Note: This is often developmental in young children.)
4. He may exhibit inadequate control of his body or clumsiness.

Educational Activities:

1. The teacher can outline the child's body on heavy construction paper, facial features, clothes, etc., and the child cuts it out.
2. Children can outline each other, cut out the figure and then try to match up the outline with the corresponding persons.
3. The children can play "Simple Simon" games.
4. The teacher can have the child lie down flat and shut his eyes. The teacher strokes one side of the child's body as he moves or otherwise indicates the corresponding part on the other side of his body.
5. He can verbalize the functions of different body parts.
6. He can have the students compare body parts to each other, to dolls, and finally to a picture of a person.
7. The teacher could use a full length mirror and stand behind the student facing the mirror and indicate body parts.
8. Pipe cleaners, clay, and wet sand are good for building figures.
9. The teacher could use activities that require the child to touch different body parts, hands, feet, etc., to different objects in the room, for example, asking students to put their right hands on all the circles and their left hands on all the squares placed around the room.

Sample Games:

1. "*Head, Shoulders, Knees, and Toes*" — The leader or teacher says the words, *Head, shoulders, knees,* and *toes* in any desired sequence. A single child or a group must then

touch the named parts in the order mentioned. The leader may state one order while demonstrating another order to see if the children can follow his spoken commands and not merely his actions. To vary this game, use different body parts and increase the number used as the ability of the children increases.

2. "Play Relay Games" — The teacher divides the students into two teams and places an object for each team to move around about twenty feet away. Then he would give each pair of students competing against each other a direction involving body parts such as "hop on one foot up and back," "hold your knees and walk up and back," or "put both hands on your head and skip up and back."

Deficits in the Area of Spatial Relationships

Observable Behaviors:

1. The learner may not be able to judge how far or how near something is in relation to himself.
2. He may not have developed "sidedness" or "laterality." This results in problems with relating oneself to an object in space.
3. He may have problems in dressing.
4. The student may have problems with directionality or object to object relationships in space. This will result in difficulty with left to right orientation.
5. He may have difficulty telling time.
6. Some learners cannot organize their thinking sequentially.
7. The student may show difficulty with placing numerals in arithmetic or in numbering down the paper for a spelling test.
8. He may have a poor sense of direction, easily getting lost and often being unable to find his way home from familiar surroundings.
9. He may have difficulty with organizing a sequence of movements necessary to carry out a specific task.
10. In some cases, this may affect the sequencing of letters or numerals causing "reversals" or inversions. More often, this is a result of poor visual sequential memory.
11. Problems with words that denote space like before, after, left, right, in between, beside, etc., may be evident.

Educational Activities:

1. The teacher can place a red arrow made out of tape on the learner's desk to remind him of the direction in which he is to proceed.
2. He can give the student clues by using color (magic markers) so that he will maintain proper placement in arithmetic. For example,

3. He can play obstacle course games with the student.

CHAP. 5   Deficit Level Curriculum

4. He can fit hands and feet into cutouts in different positions to build in handedness and laterality.
5. He can use puzzles and geometric forms.
6. Games that help the child use words that involve space such as between, in, out, etc., are good.
7. The teacher can have the student verbalize a sequence of motor acts.
8. He can let him take time to organize his thoughts.
9. He can let the student put different size cards into their respective envelopes as an exercise in spatial judgment.
10. He can ask the student to follow accurately a path bordered by blocks to aid in spatial organization.
11. He can play a game such as "How many steps do I need to take to get to the ____."

Sample Games:

1. *"Lions and Tigers"* — The players are in two groups: one called lions, the other tigers. Goal lines are marked across both ends of the playing area. Each group, in turn, stands on its goal line with the players' backs turned toward the other group. When a silent signal is given, the lions (or tigers) move quietly toward the other groups' goal line. When they are within about ten to fifteen feet, the teacher calls, "the lions (or tigers) are coming." This is the signal for the tigers (or lions) to turn and chase, until the group is safe behind their goal line. Those who were tagged before reaching the goal line go with the children of the other team and become members of that team. Repeat with the other team. This game is also good for the development of basic body movement.
2. *"Changing Partners"* — The players are grouped by twos. Partners stand back to back with elbows linked. One extra player does not have a partner. Upon a signal from the teacher, all players change while the extra player attempts to get a partner. One player will be left each time. The game is repeated with the player who is left without a partner giving the signal for the next change. This activity is also good for the development of body image.

Deficits in Balance and Coordination

Observable Behaviors:

1. The student may be clumsy or uncoordinated and appear to have poor body control.
2. He may have problems in using both sides of his body simultaneously, individually, or alternately.
3. He may use so much energy in trying to control his body that he does not pay attention to the more important aspects of learning or to what is happening in his environment.

Educational Activities:

1. The teacher can use balance beam or walking board activities.

2. He can have the student walk and balance on his toes and knees.
3. Activities such as "Rocking Horse," "Potato Race," "Crab Walk," "Frog Squat" are good.
4. The teacher can use ladder climbing activities.
5. Twist board activities are helpful.
6. The teacher can use walking, running, and jumping activities in the following ways: sideways, fast, slow, on heels, on toes, up and down steps, barefoot, squatting and shuffling.
7. He should provide for homolateral (use both arms and legs together as in pushing), unilateral (as in soldiers' walk, use of one side of the body), and cross pattern (use both sides of the body simultaneously as in walking) activities.
8. He can have the student stand, jump with legs apart, then jump pulling his feet together. This activity can be varied by having the student clap his hands over his head as he jumps with legs apart.
9. Rope and pole climbing are good exercises.

Sample Games:

1. *"Walk the Tightrope"* — A wide line is drawn on the ground and the children pretend that it is a balance beam and they are the circus performers walking on a tightrope. The children could then become more daring acrobats as they hop, skip, or jump the line. This activity is also good for the development of basic body movement and eye–foot coordination.
2. *"Duck, Duck, Goose"* — The children form a circle. One child walks around the outside of the circle touching each child on the head, saying "Duck". When he comes to a student he wants to chase him, he taps him and says "Goose". The student tapped chases the "Duck" around the circle. The "Duck" must get back to the student's place before he is tapped. If tapped, he must go into the middle of the circle. This activity is also good for the development of awareness of space and direction.
3. *"Chicken and the Egg"* — The children place their heads on the desk, with their right hand open on the desk. One child is the chicken and drops the egg (a piece of chalk) into the hand of a child who is seated. The child immediately gets up and tries to tag the chicken, who is safe if he can get back to the seat left open by the second child. This activity is also good for the development of the awareness of space and direction, eye–hand coordination, and fine muscle control.
4. *"Jack in the Box"* — The teacher or student says: "Jack is hiding down in his box until somebody opens the *lid.*" The leader says the first part very quietly and slowly in order to build suspence in the others. The children squat with their hands on their heads. This is holding the lid down on the box. The leader says the word "lid" and they all spring up and jump with their legs apart.
5. *"Camera Safari"* — The teacher asks the children if they would like to go on a "camera safari" to take pictures of animals in Africa. While the leader or teacher reads or tells the story, the children listen and follow through with appropriate actions. The story is read like this: "Let's go on a camera safari — get your camera — get your film — get your hat — put it on — duck your head when you leave the tent — get into the land rover with your guide — drive across the bumpy ground — see the tall giraffe — get your camera ready — stop the truck — focus your camera — snap the picture — drive on — stop — I see a herd of elephants — move quietly through the tall grass — tiptoe — squat down low — get your camera ready — focus — snap, etc." The teacher can give many different directions to develop movement skills.

CHAP. 5   Deficit Level Curriculum

6. "Circle Around" — Children form a circle. The teacher and children sing:

> We circle around the desks
> We circle around the room.
> We circle around the toys,
> On a Monday afternoon.
> Whoops!

Very young children circle around to the right, hands joined. When they say, "Whoops!" they all jump up in the air and then crouch down together. Older children can circle right through the first two lines, then circle left on the last two, doing the same thing on "Whoops!" The teacher can substitute the appropriate name of the day of the week.

7. "Do What I Do" — The teacher says or sings the following verse to the tune of "Old Macdonald Had a Farm" while doing some movement which the other players imitate:

> This is what I can do.
> Everybody do it too.
> This is what I can do.
> Now I send it on to you.

On the words, "Send it on to you," the teacher names, points to, or taps a student who then becomes the new leader and the game is repeated. This game can be used to further the development of body image, space and direction, balance and large muscle control.

Deficits in the Gross Motor Area

The student may have large muscle difficulties which hinder him in terms of meeting the needs of everyday life. This is especially true since our culture esteems physical agility and participation in sports.

Observable Behaviors:

1. He may be poor in sports and appear clumsy and uncoordinated.
2. He may not be able to throw a ball and appear to lose his balance easily.

Educational Activities:

1. The teacher should use swaying movements of the body whereby the learner imitates the teacher or a fellow student.
2. Games such as "Horse Walk," "Leap Frog," "See Saw," and "Pony Ride" are good.
3. The teacher can use rowing and climbing activities.
4. He can use "Touch Toes" and "Simple Simon" games.
5. He can use a large barrel open on both ends for the learner to crawl through. The barrel activity can be varied by having the teacher turn the barrel slowly as the child crawls through.
6. He can use jungle gym climbing devices.
7. A furniture dolly provides many activities and can be utilized in both the prone and seated positions.
8. The teacher can use running and jumping activities as in Item 6 of the Balance and Coordination section.

Sample Games:

1. "Call Ball" — The students stand in a circle with one child in the center. The child in the center tosses the ball above his head while calling the name or a number assigned to a child in the circle. The child whose name or number was called tries to catch the ball. This child then takes the place of the child in the center. This is also good for the development of eye—hand coordination.
2. "John Over the Ocean" — The students stand in a circle with hands joined. One player, "John," stands in the center. The students walk around in a circle chanting:

    John's over the ocean.
    John's over the sea.
    John caught a ball.
    But he can't catch me.

    As they say "me," the students squat quickly. "John" tries to tag a player before he squats down. If he is successful, the child who he tagged changes places with him and the game is repeated with a new "John." This game is also good for the development of awareness of space and direction.
3. "Catch A Fish" — Have the children sit in a circle. One child in the circle holding a large ball says, "I'm going to catch a fish!" When the fish in the center is hit, he sits in the circle. The child who has hit the fish becomes the new "fish." This activity is good for the development of the awareness of space and direction and eye—hand coordination.
4. "Stop the Ball" — Use a large ball (volleyball). The students stand in a circle with feet touching on both sides. One child is "it" and stands in the center. He tries to roll the ball through the feet of any child in the circle. If he succeeds, he takes the place of the child and this child becomes "it." Children can use only hands to stop the ball. This is also good for the development of awareness of space and direction and eye—hand coordination.
5. "Let's Play House" — Have the boys in the class "play act" various things their fathers do around the house such as fixing a flat, washing and waxing the car, working on the motor. When the leader claps his hands or gives a signal, everyone must think of another thing father does. The action chosen is then acted out. Boys would enjoy acting out other things their fathers do around the house such as sawing, mowing the lawn, or painting. Girls can play act what mother does around the house.

Deficits in Eye—Hand Coordination (Visual Motor Area)

Students with visual motor coordination problems have difficulty in getting their eyes, hands, and thought processes to work together to achieve a given task. This can also be described as a *fine motor problem*.

Observable Behaviors:

1. This is quite evident in handwriting which is often illegible.
2. The student may have problems in tasks requiring fine motor coordination such as sorting, tieing, buttoning, cutting, etc.
3. He may be clumsy with some tools and avoid these kinds of activities.

CHAP. 5 Deficit Level Curriculum

Educational Activities

General Activities:

1. The teacher can use sorting, tieing, and buttoning activities.
2. Clothespin hanging is helpful.
3. The teacher can use games such as pick-up sticks and bean-bag toss.
4. Young children can scribble with a crayon or pencil (do not overdo the activity). This can be varied with music.
5. The teacher can use sewing and lacing activities.
6. He can use peg boards and form boards.
7. Tracing activities are good.
8. Bead stringing activities with varied designs help build in better discrimination.
9. Ball bouncing and ball throwing games are good.
10. The teacher can use a nail board with rubber bands to build designs and letters.
11. He can use scissor activities with small squares of 4" by 4" heavy paper at first in the following sequence:

    a. Snipping off corners (one cut)
    b. Fringing (one cut)
    c. Fringing (two cuts without removing scissor)
    d. Cut all the way across (no lines)
    e. Cutting following a line (straight)
    f. Cutting following a line (curved)
    g. Cutting following a circle
    h. Cutting following a square
    i. Cutting following a spiral (circular)
    j. Cutting following a spiral (square)

12. The teacher can use stencils and templates.
13. Tracing folds in paper is helpful.
14. The teacher can use dot to dot tracing games.

Visual Activities:

1. The teacher faces the child and moves her finger in different directions (about two feet away) across the child's body and the child follows with his eyes without moving his head. The teacher goes slowly at first.
2. The teacher draws a line or design on the board and the child traces and follows his finger or chalk with his eyes.
3. The teacher establishes a movement pattern with a flashlight or with a pointer and the child verbalizes while visually tracking the pattern: up, down, right, left, etc.
4. A ball on a string suspended from a stick and moved across the child's body in different patterns as the student follows it with his eyes.

Sample Games:

1. "Bean Bag Toss"—Children toss bean bags into buckets or into any container with an opening. Place the container four to five feet from the children increasing the distance as the children's ability increases. Numbers may be glued on the cans. Older children can keep score.
2. "Drop the Clothespin"—From a standing position, students drop wooden clothespins into large mouth bottles or containers. Make sure they hold the clothespin at waist height when dropping the pins.
3. "Ring Toss"—Using rubber jar rings and coke bottles, or a commercial game, children throw the rings over the neck of the bottle. Here, again, numbers can be placed on the bottles and older children can keep score.

Deficits in Eye—Foot Coordination

Difficulty arises when the student cannot get his eyes, feet, and thought processes to work together automatically or otherwise to control the movements of his body. Problems in this area will affect balance and coordination.

Observable Behaviors:

Same as that for balance and coordination.

Educational Activities:

1. The teacher can have the student walk on masking tape: forward, backward, sideways, etc.
2. He can repeat number one using a balance beam.
3. He can place rope loops on the floor and have the child step into the loops.
4. Games such as "Tracing Footprints," "Hop Scotch," "Kick Ball," and "High Jump" are good.
5. The child can roll a ball with his feet to another student.
6. The teacher can have him jump over a wriggling rope.
7. He can use jump rope activities.
8. Ladder walking activities are helpful.

Sample Games:

1. "Jumping The Stream"—Two lines are drawn to represent the banks of the stream. The children run and jump over the stream. Anyone missing the jump and landing in the stream is sent "home" to put on dry shoes and socks. He sits and pretends to do these things, then reenters the game. This is also good for the development of space and direction and basic body movements.
2. "Tire Obstacle Course"—Place tires on the ground in a pattern for the children to step through. Time the children as they go through the course. Have them compete against their own best time first and later against each other.

CHAP. 5   Deficit Level Curriculum

Deficits in Body Rhythm

Observable Behaviors:

1. He may be continually out of step in marching activities.
2. This is the child that the teacher says, "Just does not do well in band or rhythm activities."
3. He may not be able to follow a rhythm in singing.

Educational Activities:

1. The teacher claps as the child moves fast and slowly, taking small, then giant steps.
2. The teacher can repeat the same activity with jumping.
3. Music activities to include marching are helpful for body rhythm.
4. The child should be allowed to use band instruments and lead the band after he has achieved reasonably good rhythm.

Sample Games:

1. "*Freeze*" — Children move to the rhythm of music, whether it be walking, swaying, turning, etc. When the music stops, they must stop or "freeze" and hold whatever position they are in until the music starts again. This is also good for the development of balance and basic body movement.
2. "*Mystery Music Leader*" — The children stand or sit in a circle. One child is selected to be "it" and leaves the room. The teacher chooses a child in the circle to be the "Mystery Music Leader." Following the beat of a metronome or rhythm stick, the leader will switch the beat from clapping to finger snapping to head nodding, etc. "It" will come back into the room and have three guesses to name the leader. The leader becomes "it" and a new child is selected to lead a new beat.

Deficits in Fine Muscle Strength (Finger Strength)

The student may lack the finger strength necessary to carry out everyday activities.

Observable Behaviors:

1. He may not be able to hold a pencil or write using fine motor movements.
2. He may not be able to use eating utensils.
3. This is related to difficulties with grasping.
4. This is often observed in the very young child who uses his whole hand to pick something up instead of using the thumb and first two fingers as in a "three draw chuck" (used in an electric drill).

Educational Activities:

1. The teacher should have the child clasp his hands and change the position of his fingers.
2. Clothespin hanging is helpful.

Language

3. He may have him squeeze a ball.
4. Working with clay is a good activity. The child can roll out the thin long snakes to be used in making letters or numerals.
5. The teacher can use snapping and clapping finger games.

Sample Game:

1. "Elephant and Peanut" — One child is selected to be the elephant. He sits on a chair in front of the children who are sitting at their desks. The elephant closes his eyes. His back is toward the other players. The elephant's peanut, which is an eraser or any small article, is placed near his chair. A child selected by the teacher attempts to sneak up to the elephant and touch and pick up his peanut without the elephant hearing him. If the elephant hears someone coming, he turns to the person and says, "Roar." Then the player must return to his own seat and another child tries. If this child is successful in touching and picking the peanut before the elephant hears him he becomes the elephant and the game is repeated. The game can be varied by adding other animal names and sounds.

Motor Development Equipment	
1. Paper and crayons	17. Blocks
2. Small chalkboards	18. Whiffle ball
3. Walking board	19. Balloons
4. Balance board	20. Magnets
5. Ladder	21. Pegboard
6. Twist board	22. Puzzles
7. Clothespins	23. Work bench
8. Small bells	24. Ring toss game
9. Masking tape	25. Clay
10. Rope	26. Beads
11. Geometric templates	27. Burlap and needles
12. Bean bags	28. Sewing and lacing boards
13. Playground ball (eight inch)	29. Finger paints
14. Ping pong ball	30. Rhythm band instruments
15. Rubber ball (three inch)	31. Tape recorder
16. Mats	

LANGUAGE

Deficits in Reception (Meaning): Visual Decoding Disorders

VISUAL LANGUAGE CLASSIFICATION PROBLEMS

Observable Behaviors:

The student with a visual language classification difficulty often cannot understand differences and sameness by category classification of objects presented visually. For example,

CHAP. 5 Deficit Level Curriculum

when the student is shown a picture of a pencil and asked whether it belongs with a picture of a pen, a ship, a hat, or a cup, he cannot discern the correct classification—the answer being in this case, a pencil belonging with a pen as both are writing tools.

Educational Activities:

1. The teacher should begin with simple activities involving concrete objects and teach difference and sameness. He can use small plastic animals or real coins, i.e., pennies, nickels, dimes, and quarters, and have the student match the coins appropriately. The child should verbalize the differences and then the sameness as he points to each grouping and physically manipulates the objects. Along with teaching difference and sameness, it is important to teach what an object is and what it is not. This must also be verbalized by the student. For example, the teacher may ask the student to show which is not a penny from among a group of coins and tell why.
2. The teacher can use color discs or blocks and repeat the same activities as with coins only color becomes the vehicle for teaching the concept of difference and sameness.
3. Difference and sameness can also be taught using as a conceptual base position, size, and shape. For example, this one is facing up, this one is shorter, this one is round, etc. The teacher should remember the objective is to build in both the understanding of the concept and the language of difference and sameness.
[Note: It is important for the teacher to determine whether or not the student has a perceptual (visual discrimination, etc.) problem to overcome in addition to a language difficulty.]
4. The next step is to teach symbols by matching in terms of difference and then sameness. The teacher should use letters and words in the form of concrete objects at first (plastic or wooden) and then printed letters and word cards.
5. The teacher should help the student look for and verbalize the common elements of concrete objects to include function. For example, pencils and pens are pointed and long; and they both are used in writing.
6. The teacher should involve the child in as much motor activity as possible. He should permit him to manipulate objects as he verbalizes difference and sameness in that order. [Note: Training should follow the sequence of activity functions listed below. This holds true for all areas of amelioration and dysfunctions. The teacher should begin at the level which is most appropriate for the individual student, using, in the various areas as necessary (a) concrete objects, (b) pictures, (c) geometric forms, and (d) symbols, i.e., letters, words, and numerals.]
7. After the student verbalizes difference and then sameness at the concrete—functional level (what it looks like and what you can do with it), the teacher should move to the abstract level using concrete objects first, then pictures. He can hold up an apple and a pear, for example, and say, "These are both round. They are both good to eat. These are both fruit." The student should do likewise. The next step would be to hold up a picture of two items and have the student give similar classifications.

Note: Many students functioning at the concrete—functional level in terms of language development do not do well with tasks that require more abstract language abilities. The vocabulary sections of the Mann-Suiter Developmental Inventories will give the teacher information as to the student's primary level of language functioning. Language in this sense becomes the "tool" of thinking or conceptualization.

Language

VISUAL LANGUAGE ASSOCIATION PROBLEMS

Observable Behaviors:

1. The student with this difficulty is unable to understand non-categorical relationships between objects presented to him visually. For example, when the student is shown a picture of bread and asked whether it belongs with a picture of butter, car, door, or a crayon, he cannot discern the correct association. In this case, it is bread and butter.
2. The student may not be able to associate a word he can read with the appropriate unit of experience. This type of student is sometimes referred to as a "word caller." He can read, but does not understand.
3. The student's verbal and/or written language and arithmetic may also be affected by this disorder in that he may not be able to associate words and/or numerals that he sees with meaning.

Educational Activities:

1. The teacher can build the student's vocabulary by beginning with words within his experience.
2. He should begin with concrete objects (for example, an apple), and have the student match the oral word with the single object first. Then he should ask the student to match the word with the appropriate object picked from a group of three or four objects. ("Give me an apple.")
3. The teacher should have the student match oral words with pictures of objects within his experience. He should begin with single words and match them to pictures and then let the student match the word with the appropriate picture picked from a group of three or four different pictures.
4. The teacher holds up familiar objects and the student describes the objects in terms of quality and function. The student should be allowed to manipulate the objects as he describes them.
5. The teacher holds up pictures of familiar objects and the student does the same as with the concrete objects mentioned above.
6. The teacher should try to get short phrase or short sentence responses from the student if he cannot give a long sentence, for example, "cotton," "soft cotton," "The cotton is soft."
7. The teacher should have the student follow directions that he has given by pointing or showing. For example, the teacher points to the door and motions for the student to close it.

(Note: The teacher must slow down the rate and amount of input for all activities accordingly to avoid frustration.)

Auditory Decoding Disorders

AUDITORY LANGUAGE CLASSIFICATION PROBLEMS

Observable Behaviors:

The student with an auditory language classification difficulty often cannot understand difference and sameness by category classification of objects presented orally. For example, when

CHAP. 5   Deficit Level Curriculum

a student is asked whether a puppy belongs with ship, hat, door, or dog, he cannot discern the correct classification of puppy belonging with dog.

Educational Activities:

1. The teacher should begin with simple auditory activities to teach the concept of difference and sameness. He should be sure the student verbalizes what the sound is as well as what it is not. The following sequence is recommended:
   a. Gross sounds—bells, drums, dogs, etc. Teach different and same for gross sounds first. (Between bells and drums) Then by classification. (all bells and all drums)
   b. Gross sound recognition—play records of different sounds and ask the student to identify the sounds.
   c. Contrasting gross sounds—ask the student to tell you which is loud, louder, loudest, low, lower, lowest, high, higher, highest, etc. Vary sounds in frequency, intensity, pitch, and timbre. Try to get complete sentence responses if you can. Remember to have the student verbalize what is loud as well as what is not loud.
   d. Help the student identify beginning sounds of words which are different and alike, then ending sounds which are different and alike, and finally, medial sounds which are the most difficult to discern.
2. The teacher should use classification analysis games. For example, the teacher says one word such as "ball." The student names as many types of balls as he can, such as football, baseball, and handball.
3. The teacher can engage the student in category games:
   a. Which one does not belong? A cat, a dog, an umbrella.
   b. What are all of these called together? A pear, a plum, a peach.
   c. How many vegetables can you name?

AUDITORY LANGUAGE ASSOCIATION PROBLEMS

Observable Behaviors:

1. The student with this difficulty is unable to understand non-categorical relationships between words presented orally. For example when the student is asked whether a motor belongs with a door, water, lamp, or car, he cannot discern the correct association of motor with car.
2. A child with an association problem may have difficulty in deriving meaning from words. He can hear, but cannot associate words with meaning and therefore, does not understand.
3. He may have difficulty in relating the spoken and/or written word with the appropriate unit of experience.

(Note: Sometimes this disorder in its severity is referred to as childhood aphasia.)

4. He may be frustrated by conversation.
5. Difficulty may be evident with descriptors such as adjectives and adverbs.
6. Verbal expression or spoken language is often affected as well as reading, writing, and arithmetic. He may not be able to carry out a series of directions (check auditory memory).

Language

7. These children have a great deal of difficulty with figurative language. For example, the student may not understand the concept of the "underground railroad" during the Civil War or such statements as "he was chewed out" or "he has had it."
8. The student may not be able to associate the "m" sound in mother with the "m" sound in man causing him difficulty in learning phonics. He may not transfer the sound of "m" in one word to the sound of "m" in another word (check auditory memory). This is a critical skill for success in the first grade. This is also known as an auditory-to-auditory language association problem.
9. The student may not be able to associate the sound of "m" with the symbol "m." This is also called an auditory-to-visual association language problem and is another one of the critical skills necessary for success in first-grade language arts.

Educational Activities:

1. The teacher should make the student aware of sound by beginning with sound as opposed to no-sound activities. The teacher asks the student to raise his hand when he hears the sound of machines turned on or off.
2. The teacher should use activities where the student has to identify the source of sounds—first with his eyes open and then with his eyes shut.
3. The teacher should use phoneme association games such as: think of a word that begins like *boy* and sounds like *tag*.
4. The teacher can build in appropriate affectional association and improve social perception by varying the emotional tone of the verbal responses to include: anger, excitement, declaration, interrogation, apathy, and happiness.
    a. He can use puppets and carry on a dialogue that expresses the gamut of emotions. After the dialogue, the student can select from a group of pictures the facial expressions that the puppets expressed.
    b. He can play a record of verbal behavior expressing emotions. The teacher stands behind the student as they both look into a full length mirror. As the emotions are expressed, the student and the teacher pattern or pantomine the behavior. A full length mirror is good for developing social preception and language.

Note: These activities are also applicable to visual language association problems.

5. Matching games should be used to include the following:
    a. Environmental sounds such as horns with concrete objects and with pictures of horns.
    b. Animal sounds with pictures of animals.
    c. Words with concrete objects and then with pictures of objects.
    d. Words given orally with words printed on cards.
6. The teacher can collect and use records of rhyming words and let the student hear difference and then sameness.
7. The teacher should build vocabulary beginning with words within the student's experience only.
8. In the beginning, the teacher should ask short questions requiring short one-concept answers.
9. The teacher says a word. He tells the child to clap his hands when he hears the correct word among other words.

CHAP. 5 Deficit Level Curriculum

10. The student should be trained to describe from memory, "What does an apple look like," "what does your room look like," etc.
11. The teacher should begin with simple nouns and use concrete objects, then use pictures of objects. He should show the object and discuss as follows:
    a. The quality of an object—for example, the pencil is hard. Then remove the object from sight and discuss what the child has learned immediately.
    b. The action potential of an object—for example, the pencil is used to write with, etc. The student then describes from memory what he has learned.
12. The teacher should build in a sequence of phrases with action words that are associated with one noun first, for example, the boy walks, the boy runs, the boy eats, etc.
13. The intent of these activities is for the student to verbalize associations between objects. He should be able to do this eventually without the object present as well as he can with the object present. Games that involve symbol or object associations will enable the student to "see" relationships more readily. For example,
    a. The "what-goes-with-what" type of games, such as "What goes with shoe?"
    b. "Does bird go with feather, iron, or mountain?"
    c. The "what-is-the-opposite-of" type games: "What is the opposite of big?" "What is the opposite of high?" "What is the opposite of in?" etc.
14. The teacher can ask the student simple riddles. For example, "What is white and hard and you can write on the chalkboard with it?"
15. The teacher can ask association type questions about stories read to the student and about TV programs they are both watching.
16. He can teach cause–effect associations by asking the students such questions as:
    a. "When you see dark clouds in the sky, and lightning and thunder, what will happen?"
    b. "Why can't dogs fly?"

Disorders of Expression

DEFICITS IN MOTOR LANGUAGE EXPRESSION:
Manual (Hand, or foot)
The student is unable to express manually the function of an object even though when asked, he may be able to identify it from among other objects. For example, the student may be able to identify a hammer from among other objects but not be able to show what to do with it manually.

Educational Activities:

1. The teacher should begin with real objects within the student's experience.
    a. Find out if the student knows the functions and movements of parts of his own body. The teacher demonstrates first on his own body. The student imitates the teacher and verbalizes the functions. For example, "My hands can hold, give, write, hit, stroke, clap," etc. "My eyes can open, close, see, blink, wink, squint, move from side to side, and up and down," etc.
    b. Use things he is familiar with such as a pencil, which can write, poke, erase, tickle, scratch, roll, etc.
    c. Use things the student can manipulate. Other objects can include cars, fishing poles, footballs, pans, string, bucket, paper clips, a door, or a hose.

Language

Note: The process in teaching is *imitation* (do as I do), *understanding* (show me the one that writes, for example, from among three objects), then *elicited responses* (show me what this does). The teacher should teach the object, the word, and the function simultaneously beginning with the concrete first, then going to pictures. (Some cautionary advice: Proceed slowly! Do not "jam" the child with too much too fast. Leave him with a success.)

2. The teacher can pantomime the motion of hammering a nail and the student has to pick up the real object (a hammer) from among three or four objects.

Note: The above activities should also develop creativity as well as improve the language abilities of the student.

SPEECH

Observable Behaviors:

1. The student may exhibit poor speech patterns and be unable to say words.
2. He has difficulty in retrieving the motor act of speech even if he is provided with a model or he can comprehend and recall.
3. He may have problems with execution or articulation, exhibiting omissions (leaving out initial, medial, or final sounds), substitutions (*wabbit* for *rabbit*), distortions (lisp, sloppy "s" or a hissing sound), or additions (*sumber* for *summer*) of sounds and words.
4. He may use gestures and pantomime a great deal.
5. In some cases, the tongue appears to be lost in the mouth during speech.
6. Difficulty will be observed in being able to *imitate* words regardless of whom the child is attempting to model.

Educational Activities:

1. The teacher should make the child aware of sounds and the movements of the organs of speech by
   a. Using mirrors to illustrate positioning.
   b. Using touch to feel positioning as letters and words are formed (hands on face and throat).
2. He can use visual clues to include
   a. Follow-the-leader games, i.e., look listen, and imitate.
   b. Blowing, smiling, licking, and tongue movement activities are good.
   c. Peanut butter put in different places in the mouth will facilitate better tongue placement.
3. The teacher should establish a motor pattern by introducing sounds (c a t), reinforcing them with touch (feeling the organs of speech), and then converting them into a word (verbalization) by saying the word *cat*.
4. The teacher should give the student specific verbal directions as to how to produce the sound or word. An example would be to "open your mouth, purse your lips, and blow," or "place your tongue between your teeth and force air through the opening," etc.
5. He can experiment with tactual–kinesthetic associations.

CHAP. 5   Deficit Level Curriculum

      a. The teacher would use a tongue depressor or lollipop to guide placement of the tongue.
      b. The teacher should overarticulate while the student feels the teacher's face.
      c. The student should feel his own face and throat as he speaks.
6. The teacher should repeat the word correctly at first without correcting the student each time.

DEFICITS IN VERBAL LANGUAGE EXPRESSION. The student may be able to identify a hammer from among other objects presented visually. He may be able to show what can be done with it but be unable to talk about it in a meaningful way, or to describe its function.

Note: Language reception must be checked first since receptive disorders will invariably affect expression. The teacher must begin by finding out if the child understands the word (intact reception). This can be done by giving the student alternatives to choose from. Is this a crayon? Is this a hat? Is this chalk? If chalk is the object and the student responds correctly, then the teacher can surmise that he probably has an expressive language problem and not a receptive language disorder.

PROBLEMS WITH WORD RETRIEVAL

Observable Behaviors:

1. The student exhibits difficulty in recalling or retrieving words for use in speaking.
2. He may not be able to express himself in a complete sentence.
3. He may be able to repeat immediately after he hears a letter or word but be unable to recall after somewhat longer periods of time.
4. He may use gestures and vocalization often to make wants known.
5. Retrieving words can sometimes be achieved when seeing or feeling the concrete object.
6. He can generally read better silently than orally.
7. He may have non-fluent speech that includes hesitations which appear like stuttering.
8. He may not be able to sequence his thoughts or ideas.
9. He may use word substitutions such as a "whatchamacallit," or a "thingamajig," or "gismo."
10. He may emit strange sounds for words such as "I foga da shugum" for "I swallowed the chewing gum." Find out if he can imitate the correct pronunciation.

Educational Activities:

Note: The teacher must slow down the rate and amount of input. He should wait for a response and not rush the student. The teacher should reduce his demands for spoken language at first.

1. He should give him clues, say, "do you mean," or give him the first letter of the word.

Language

2. He should have the child imitate single words presented verbally first, and associate them with an object, then a picture, for example, chalk (object–picture), pencil, etc. Then the teacher should add qualifiers (adjectives and adverbs) in short phrases, next sentences using objects then pictures of objects, for example, "Chalk is hard. I write with chalk," etc.
3. He should use cueing, such as "I write with a ____."
4. He should use associative ideas, such as pairing: i.e., "bread and ____," "salt and ____."
5. He should get the student to verbalize opposites and similarities of objects, then pictures.
6. He should encourage the child to use words instead of gestures and try to elicit short phrase responses, then sentences.

PROBLEMS WITH SYNTAX AND FORMULATION. Students with this difficulty have problems with the smooth and natural flow of the English language. They cannot structure their thoughts into grammatically correct verbal units or sentences.

Observable Behaviors:

1. He may understand what you say but answers in single words or phrases with inadequate language structure.
2. Syntax may be poor in that he may omit words, distort the order of words, or use poor tense.
3. He may recognize correct sentence structure but cannot reproduce a meaningful sequence himself.
4. He may use telegraphic speech, i.e., mom–dad–me–go, in attempting to formulate a sentence.
5. This student often has difficulty in expressing ideas or formulating sentences by using words.

Educational Activities:

1. The teacher should have the student verbalize his actions during meaningful play.
2. He should use pictures and have the child name the object. He should use the word in a sentence and then develop a sequence of sentences about the object.
3. The teacher can elicit a response from the student by saying sentences, leaving out a word, and having the child supply the missing word, for example, "I have a ____ ball."
4. He can scramble words and then build sentences using word cards.
5. He can use sequential pictures such as comic strips, or sequence puzzles, and have the student verbalize the sequence of actions.
6. The teacher makes sequence puzzles based on simple stories or themes and has the student order them.
7. Ordering or sequence of thought can be taught by giving the student two sentences in different order and asking him to give the correct sequence. For example,

    I ate my breakfast.
    I got up in the morning.
8. A sequence of amelioration activities such as follows may be helpful:
    a. *Restructuring verbal responses (imitation)*—The student first repeats short, verbalized sentences given by the teacher indicating the correct tense. For example,

CHAP. 5   Deficit Level Curriculum

> Look at me.
> He looked at me.
> He is looking at me.

The teacher can use the same sentences again substituting different pronouns, i.e., we, she, etc., or children's names. This activity can be reinforced by using associative clues such as pictures or film strips.

b. *Understanding*—The student can indicate understanding by responding to (1) actions, (2) emotions, and (3) cause–effect relationships. For example, the student is asked questions based on pictures of *actions* (a boy running), *emotions* (a girl crying), and *cause–effect* relationships (a boy falling) that reflect the appropriate tense.

Sample Activity: Understanding the verb *fall*. Show the student three pictures:

> A boy running.
> A boy tripping over a stone and falling.
> A boy on the ground.

The teacher says, "Show me the picture that means the boy is falling." The student repeats the sentence and indicates his understanding by selecting the correct response (if incorrect, repeat as necessary until understood). The same thing is done with the picture of the boy on the ground. The teacher says, "Show me the picture that means the boy has fallen."

c. *Elicited Responses*—In this activity, the teacher provides a stimulus picture indicating (1) an action, (2) an emotion, and (3) a cause–effect relationship.

Sample Activity: In expressing the verb *eat*, for example, the teacher shows the student a series of cards one at a time of a puppy standing over a full bowl, a puppy eating, and a puppy standing over an empty bowl. The teacher asks, "What is the puppy doing?" for each of these pictures. The student may reply with one word, a phrase, or a sentence. With practice one word and phrase responses should develop into sentences. The teacher should always repeat the response in a complete sentence even though the student may answer in one word. Vary the activities by having the teacher give the first sentences in a sequence and the student give the next one or two sentences.

DEFICITS WITH WRITTEN EXPRESSIVE LANGUAGE

Observable Behaviors:

1. Individuals with problems in oral expressive language tend to write the way they speak.
2. Those with retrieval problems are less consistent in their written errors than are those with difficulties in formulation. They may be unable to recall the visual image of a word that they cannot recall auditorily, and their written work may be somewhat better than their spoken language.

Educational Activities:

1. Many of the educational procedures listed in the preceding sections could be used in the remediation of written language disorders. The only substitution would be to use written instead of oral exercises. Most of the work should involve the child at the particular level of his reading program and not his writing or speaking program.

2. The teacher can have the student write sentences and read them aloud. When he identifies an error, the teacher should provide a written model for him so that he can make the corrections on his paper.
3. The next step is to have him monitor his own written work by having him read it aloud to himself, checking every work as he says it. Much later, he will learn to reauditorize to himself while scrutinizing printed words.
4. The teacher can write sentences containing one, then two errors, and ask the student if the one he hears is the same as the one he sees on a correct copy. For example, teacher reads one at a time:
John went the story yesterday.
The girl fell off him bicycle.
Tomorrow we swimming in the pond.
While the student's correct copy contains:
John went to the store yesterday.
The girl fell off her bicycle.
Tomorrow we will go swimming in the pond.
5. The student can be given a group of word cards which must be arranged in the order spoken by the teacher, i.e., "The children are going to school." The student first arranges the words in the proper order and then copies the cards.

EXPRESSIVE LANGUAGE PROBLEMS IN ARITHMETIC

Observable Behaviors:

1. Problems with retrieval will keep the child from quickly recalling numbers. He may recognize the correct number when he sees it but be unable to say the one he wants. Rapid oral drills are difficult for him and should be avoided until he has improved in retrieval.
2. He may not be deficient in understanding quantitative relationships and may do quite well in computation as long as it is written and not oral.

Educational Activities:

1. All oral work in both computation and problem solving should be reinforced by the "open channel," i.e., tactual, and/or visual while the deficit area is being strengthened.
2. See Chapter 8 on arithmetic problems.

Non-Verbal Language Problems

Students with a non-verbal language difficulty have problems with assigning meaning to such non-verbal functions as art, religion, music, holidays, or patriotism. There is a language of art and music from which the individual cannot derive meaning. Often, this disorder is accompanied by problems in the spatial area.

Observable Behaviors:

1. He may have difficulty with judgment of quantity, i.e., size, time, shape, and distance as well as with seasons of the year.

CHAP. 5   Deficit Level Curriculum

2. He may not be able to understand religious symbols such as a "Star of David, "Cross," or a "Crescent Moon."
3. He may not understand the significance of the statue of "Iwo Jima" or the "Washington Monument."
4. Although his verbal language may be quite good, or even superior, he appears to have difficulty in formulating good judgment about things that are symbolic in nature.
5. He may also exhibit difficulty with social perception involving non-verbal relationships with people.

Educational Activities:

1. The teacher should begin by talking about things in the child's own environment. Does he keep things that he feels will bring him luck, such as a rabbit's foot or a special toy.
2. He can talk about how we remember people, include monuments, statues, tombstones, etc.
3. He can begin with a simple painting or a patriotic song and talk about how the person may have felt when he painted it or wrote it such as Francis Scott Key and the *Star Spangled Banner*.
4. The teacher and the student make a list of pictures and objects that have symbolic significance and have the student verbalize the relationships.
5. He can ask the student to match a list of holidays with the appropriate objects and pictures.
6. He can talk about the history of particular symbols in the student's environment. How did flags as symbols begin? Are there other symbols for countries or people, i.e., shields, seals, crests, etc.
7. He can have the student design and name his own family crest if he has the ability to do so.
8. He can have students collect, label, and discuss emblems and badges representing different social organizations such as scouting, the Armed Services, and local clubs.

Inner-Language Disorders

Inner-language is the language with which one thinks. Inner-language serves to integrate experiences associated with a native spoken language. This can also be thought of as inner-speech. Inner-speech in this sense relates to thinking while outer-speech serves to provide for communication between people.

Observable Behaviors:

1. Some types of inner-language difficulties are a result of cerebral dysfunction.
2. An inner-language conflict may result when the student has incorporated as his native language a language other than standard English and cannot or will not integrate standard English as a functional language. This other language can be sign language, a foreign language, or a dialect as found in different cultures.
3. The student may think or solve problems in his native language even though he can speak fluent standard English.

4. He may, however, have three different sounds for the same phonetic construct; an example in point is the student who may say, "bafroom" for "bathroom," "mover" for "mother," and "da" for "the," all indicating three different sounds for "th".
5. Some students have internalized the phonetic or sound system of a foreign language and have difficulty in learning the English phoneme-grapheme system.

Educational Activities:

1. In teaching initial reading, the learner should be given the best model possible. The words must be said correctly by the teacher and elicited from the student correctly at least one time no matter how he wishes to pronounce it later on.
2. It is important not to correct his speech constantly as he probably will incorporate standard English speech patterns when he is ready to do so.
3. The student must be told explicitly that there is a universal English phonetic system common to all English speaking people. For communication purposes, this must be learned. This will hold true for purposes of verbal communication as well as reading and writing. Otherwise, he must teach his code to anyone who doesn't know it with whom he wishes to communicate. He must understand for example that there is a voiced and unvoiced "th" and that this is constant regardless of how he wishes to pronounce it verbally. He should also learn that different people have different pronunciations for the same words, but they are all the same sounds in reading.
4. The student should be taught that there is a language of the home, the school, and of literature. He must learn to use each one appropriately.
5. The teacher should build on words based on the student's experiences first, and give the student many opportunities to verbalize his feelings and experiences. Teachers sometimes tend to talk too much. Remember, the sequence in learning is verbal, reading, and then writing. Activities under syntax and formulation are appropriate here.
6. The teacher should remember the sound "t" is not "tuh"; He should not add a vowel to a consonant when saying the sound as this adds to the confusion.
7. The teacher should talk about the history of language and how people learned to communicate with each other both verbally and non-verbally.
8. He should develop activities that involve the student in creating his own code so that he can see more readily the function of communication.

CONTROL FACTORS

Factors that affect control are those behaviors that originate from within the student and/or are precipitated by stimuli in the environment. These factors cause the student to exhibit atypical behavior or behavior that hinders him in terms of school adjustment and the acquisition of new concepts.

Distractability

Observable Behaviors:

1. The student exhibits "Forced Attention" to extraneous stimuli within his environment and cannot attend to the task.

CHAP. 5   Deficit Level Curriculum

2. He may respond to the teacher next door and follow his directions.
3. Distractability can accompany deficits in the sensory, perceptual, memory, or language levels of learning or be related to emotional problems.
4. He may be distracted by visual or auditory stimulus or both.

Educational Activities:

1. The teacher should reduce the input or stimulus in the room.
2. He should provide a place to "escape" from distraction.
3. He should put the distraction (color, etc.) into the material rather than on the walls.
4. The teacher should condition the learner by building in distraction (materials, bulletin board, etc.) a little at a time.
5. Involving the student in a motor act often reduces distraction. Manipulative materials such as clay, sand, wooden letters, felt letters, and finger paints are good.

Disinhibition

Observable Behaviors:

1. This is the learner who gets carried away by his own thoughts.
2. He may give inappropriate responses that are unrelated to the question asked.
3. He cannot put on his "braking mechanisms," or control himself.

Educational Activities:

1. The teacher can help the child stay on the task or idea by touching him or by using such "breaking words" as "no" or "wait."
2. He can give him something to do with his hands (manipulatives).
3. He should be calm and not appear irritated when giving directions.
4. He should reward "on task" behavior and not reward in any fashion inappropriate behavior.

Perseveration

Observable Behaviors:

1. In verbal behavior, the learner may say a word over and over.
2. He cannot shift from one activity to another.
3. On tests, he tends to repeat the previous response.
4. In arithmetic, he may add all the problems even though he can easily see that half of them are subtraction.

Educational Activities:

1. The child must learn to listen, wait, and then respond correctly.

2. Perseveration can be broken in many cases with a motor act. For example,
John draws this — ◯
The teacher says, "John, give me your eraser"
(motor act)
Now John, draw this — ☐
3. Another technique is to go to something else and then come back to the next task.
4. Red lines as a key to a change in directions or process are helpful for the student with this difficulty.

Social Perception

Observable Behaviors:

1. He may misinterpret what he sees and give you the wrong response.
2. He may have difficulty with projective tests such as the "Thematic Apperception Test" (L. Bellak 1954).
3. He may be able to perceive individual objects but fails in comprehending the meaning of their relationships.
4. The student may not derive meaning from gestures or expressions.
5. He may not be able to "size up a situation." For example, he may require constant interpretation while watching a TV show.
6. The teacher should look for the learners who literally do not know enough to come in out of the rain. Too often, they are directed at home and rarely have opportunities to make up their own mind.

Educational Activities:

1. The teacher can train the child through the interpretation of good pictures or photographs. He should be careful not to overstimulate the child with too much input and should begin with simple pictures.
2. He should show the student action pictures.
3. The teacher can train the child with sequence pictures or comic strips — record the child's responses and lead him through by asking questions.
4. The teacher can build in good social perception through language experience utilizing the science curriculum and by helping the student understand cause – effect relationships.

MOTIVATIONAL AND EMOTIONAL FACTORS

Acting Out Behavior

Behavior which could be described as being "acting out" in nature seems to be an effect of many factors. The following are a few examples of such factors.

1. *Coping with boredom.* The learner may become bored with school because he has a

CHAP. 5   Deficit Level Curriculum

processing problem, is not learning, and cannot cope with the instructional program and the materials which may be beyond his grasp. Learners who are gifted often complete their work easily and before the rest of the students. If the teacher is not prepared to give this student enriching kinds of activities he may get bored with nothing else to do, resulting in noxious or annoying behavior. Indeed, there are a number of children who are neither learning handicapped nor gifted who, through lack of stimulation, in school, exhibit boredom with its concomitant behavioral difficulties.

2. *The phenomenon of natural movement.* The teacher must understand the fact that children must move and tend to wrestle or otherwise engage in body contact with each other as part of the natural developmental growth process. The "anxious" teacher who makes a "mountain out of a mole hill" in these situations may create problems where none may exist.

3. *Dealing with authority figures.* Some students feel the need to engage in a personal battle with adults whether they be parents, teachers, or others who may represent authority figures. Recent events in our culture related to the activity of youth and the notoriety given this activity by the media in terms of campus behavior, demonstrations, and physical appearance, etc. have given further impetus to this kind of behavior in even younger learners.

4. *Coping with panic and anxiety.* Panic-coping is probably one of the most critical areas of concern pertaining to the student who exhibits a processing problem or a learning disability. Pressure from parents, teachers, and peers can result in a continual state of frustration with accompanying anxiety. This anxiety can become specifically associated with a particular learning task such as reading, writing, or arithmetic. The student who fails in reading and at the same time receives a great deal of pressure to learn to read from books may become anxious and tense when asked to read from a book or even generalize this anxiety to all books. Perhaps children who are "book anxious" need to be taught to read away from books completely and should be given the book only when they can achieve 100% success in terms of the reading vocabulary of a particular volume.

5. *The need to be heard.* Some learners have a desperate desire to be heard and require a great deal of attention and "eye contact." Most teachers do not have the time to give to the learner with this problem and may find that the student will do almost anything to get the teacher's attention or to engage in conversation. Attention-getting behaviors may take a negative form and the student may begin disturbing other learners, making strange noises, breaking things, interrupting the teacher, and doing the myriad of other things that can be considered noxious.

6. *Testing limits.* Many experienced teachers have learned that it is almost axiomatic that children will test limits in terms of interpersonal relationships. Sometimes opportunities for testing limits in different situations are not readily available in the home or community. In many instances where they are available in the student's out-of-school life, individuals who are important to him may not be consistent in the way they permit or react to testing. Children are generally uncomfortable with ambiguity or inconsistency and will force the teacher to deal or not to deal with different kinds of behaviors. It is the way the teacher deals with testing behaviors both initially and continually that makes the difference in many cases between rapport and constant hassling in the learning environment.

7. *Peer group loyalty.* Today, teachers are even more aware of peer group loyalties in children than perhaps in previous years. This may be due to the effects of recent changes within our society in terms of the behavior of young people and especially with respect to minority group activity to achieve equal educational opportunities. This goes beyond the "I'll show you I'm brave and not chicken" kind of loyalty that commonly exists which, to some extent, has always existed as a developmental phenomenon in the pro-

Motivational and Emotional Factors

cess of the growth of young people. Today, however, although this attitude is being observed more and more in individuals in the elementary schools, in many instances it has taken on the veil of "cultural overtness" vis-a-vis "I am a free soul" or "I am black" or "I am Chicano and I am proud of it, and I will indicate this to you in any way that I can because you are a member of an established order or system that has been traditionally against me and mine."

Teachers in many situations have become fearful of students and have come to misunderstand this form of exhibiting group loyalties to mean hostility that is directed toward the teacher personally. In some instances it is hostility, and it is directed toward the teacher; however, if it is treated as hostility and returned in kind, it can result in unfortunate and unhappy situations for all involved.

Withdrawing Behavior

Many children with learning problems become withdrawn or learn to "play the game." Others isolate themselves from learning and from people. A few things to consider in these situations are as follows:

1. *Investment of self.* The student will need to invest of himself and learn to tolerate more frustration. In return for his investment he must achieve success. After a failure, the teacher must be certain that the student is taken back to a success level for a particular task and that the input is regulated to be consistent with his rate of learning.
2. *Evasive maneuvers.* Sometimes this type of student becomes the best errand runner in the class. He will do anything to avoid academic work. The teacher must take care not to give the student too many opportunities to avoid task related activities. Small increments of success must be pointed out to the student so that he will have something to strive for. Perhaps the "stomach aches" and "headaches," or "I don't feel goods" will subside if the learner has something which he can look forward to. It is difficult to give hope to a student who has lost hope because everyone in his life has labeled him a "loser," perhaps not with words but certainly with actions. The withdrawn child, it appears, may have many more problems to overcome than the one who is "acting out." The "acting out" learner is still, in most cases, fighting to survive, while the "withdrawn" learner may have already given up hope. It will take the combined effort of the school, the home, and the community in dealing with the total learner to facilitate any real changes in the behavior of these children.
3. *Playing the game.* Some students pretend to "play the game" and appear to be busy and occupied with the task as indicated by the teacher. The student who is holding the book may be doing just that and nothing else. Therefore, in defining task-related behavior, it is important to be certain that it is "functional" rather than "non-functional," task-related behavior.

Modifying Learner Behavior

1. "Know thyself teacher." It is difficult to be what you are not. As an individual responsible for children the teacher needs to ask himself such questions as "what sets me off or gets me uptight as a person?" Research has not indicated that one type of personality, a "permissive" person, for example, makes a better teacher than a person who is consid-

CHAP. 5   Deficit Level Curriculum

ered a "disciplinarian." It is difficult to ask a laissez-faire, permissive type of individual to suddenly change his way of life and become well-disciplined and structured, or vice versa. However, understanding oneself may result in a teacher being more ready to understand the behavior of learners in terms of their conduct being essentially an effect of their total experiences, rather than something that is just directed at the person in authority.

2. The teacher should begin by establishing guidelines and structuring the environment. This means the teacher needs to delineate to the learners at the start of the school year not only the dynamics of the learning environment in terms of their role, but, more importantly, the teacher's role both as an educator and as a human being. Young learners tend to see teachers as something "extra human." So do many parents. The students should understand that the teacher has "bad days" and "good days" and that he will exhibit anger and frustration as well as happiness and understanding. The teacher, at the same time, can indicate that he will try not to impose his personal unhappiness on the students, but, being human, situations could occur; and he would need the understanding of those around him. The reverse side of the coin will also hold true and the teacher should indicate that he will try to be understanding when a student has a "bad day" and will indicate this to the student.

3. Rapport may be difficult or almost impossible to obtain with some children. In any case, the learner must be told explicitly (use good judgment) after a crisis situation that although his behavior threatens the entire learning situation it will not be taken as a personal battle between him and the teacher. This tends to put the situation or episode on a more objective level. The teacher must permit testing within reasonable limits but should not allow aberrant behavior to go beyond the established guidelines, especially letting it continue until tempers flair. In other words, don't wait five minutes until the situation gets completely out of hand before you step in. Know how far you can go with each child. A pat on the shoulder can send one student off on a rampage. Another child may need a great deal of "mothering" and "body contact." This is where reading the cumulative records and talking to the previous teachers is so important. This information should not only tell you what to do but what not to do with a particular student. The earlier in the year you get this information the easier it will be for all parties concerned.

4. The teacher may have to begin with "non-school types of activities" in order to win the student back to learning. These include many of the readiness games at different levels which appear to be "play" but in reality are task-oriented. Some students have been "turned off" for too long. They should be introduced to formal academics gradually.

5. Reinforcement or punishment should not be postponed for long periods of time. Punishment, regardless of form, may get so far removed from the particular incident that it becomes meaningless.

6. The teacher should not get into a "social drama" with the student by backing him up against the wall with such statements as, "If you do that one more time you will leave my room and never come back." Few administrators will support such a statement and many students know this. It may result in your losing the respect of the other learners in the class. It is better to speak to the learner in private and agree on some strategy that will result in your both being better able to work together. During the student-teacher conference it may be decided to include other people to help solve the problem, such as a counselor, the principal, parents, or even other teachers whose advice and objectivity may help improve the situation.

7. The teacher should provide for group and individual opportunities to express feelings in a non-threatening environment. This can be accomplished by the teacher through struc-

tured group and individual counseling programs or by a counselor or psychologist, should one be available. Homeroom counseling after school may be the best time to listen to students and work out problems.
8. A good behavior reinforcement or behavior modification program can be established whereby the individual is rewarded for successive approximations for a given task. The teacher should reward on-task behavior for example and should not in any way (positively or negatively) reinforce negative behavior. A few of the more commonly used techniques include
   a. Different colored stars to be later exchanged for toys, school supplies, or opportunities to play in a pleasant setting.
   b. Token reinforcement, later to be exchanged for tangible rewards.
   c. A "time" or "clock stamp" can be used with a time clock. The teacher stamps small pieces of paper with the clock stamp, and the number of minutes of on-task behavior is marked as indicated by the time clock that is left on the student's desk. The teacher then will write in the minute and hour hands that will indicate the amount of time that the student has worked at a particular task. This is later tallied and "time" is exchanged for tangible rewards.

The important thing to remember is that although the material rewards are good, in many cases they will have limited transfer value. Success at the academic task must become rewarding in and of itself. Therefore, the teacher must provide for a success mode in the learning environment.

9. The teacher might begin establishing better school–home relationships by sending home only that which the student can accomplish at his independent level. Another suggestion is to reduce or eliminate altogether the sending home of "red marked" poor papers which may further lead to poor parent–child–teacher relationships. The teacher should notify the parent through a telephone call or a short note when the learner has experienced success in school either in academic tasks or in his social-emotional behavior.

Summary

Learners can achieve success if the rate, amount, and sequence of input are regulated appropriately. It becomes the task of the teacher to decode the student in both the cognitive and affective areas, so that truly individualized programs can be instituted. In a real sense the primary purpose of school is to serve children. This is a most difficult concept for many teachers to understand. The school belongs to the learners and not to the educators.

CHAPTER 6

TASK LEVEL CURRICULUM

Students exhibiting difficulties in the language arts and arithmetic areas will require a modified curriculum which considers both strengths and weaknesses in their abilities to process information. The suggested approaches to teaching reading, handwriting, spelling, and arithmetic in this chapter will enable the instructor to develop a more systematic curriculum in teaching these students. A good deal of attention is given to breaking down these specific tasks into their basic components. This will enable the instructor to better understand the nature of the task and to focus upon the particular levels on which the student may be presently functioning.

Curriculum suggestions are made in the following task-level (language arts and arithmetic) areas: (1) reading, (2) spelling, (3) handwriting, (4) language, and (5) arithmetic.

READING: INITIAL AND REMEDIAL TEACHING APPROACHES

In examining the task of reading, we find many interrelated factors. Children, to become effective readers, must be able to

1. see a clear and unblurred image on a white field and hear the sounds of the letters and words (auditory–visual sensory input)
2. distinguish one symbol from another and recognize these differences consistently (auditory–visual perception)
3. remember the sounds or images of the symbols in sequence (auditory–visual memory)
4. relate these symbols to meaning based on experience and synthesize the visual and auditory clues with the meaningful words for integrative learning (language–symbolization)
5. do all of these things smoothly and with reasonable efficient speed (input–output relationships).

Reading is a dynamic process in which perception, memory, language, and affect must function harmoniously with each other. Many educators feel that a unitary approach to teaching reading cannot be used for children exhibiting a variety of learning deficits.

CHAP. 6 Task Level Curriculum

Remedial plans must take into consideration the patterns of the student's strengths and weaknesses.

The recommendations made here are based upon a theoretical approach to instruction which focuses upon the needs of specific children or groups of children manifesting similar characteristics and problems. The teacher must be aware of and program for the learner's disabilities as well as his strengths. The strategy for remediation includes circumventing the major area of deficit for instructional purposes while simultaneously including work in the deficit areas. Since the same methodologies cannot be applied to every child, the teacher needs to adjust the program accordingly.

Even after the teacher has formed a basic philosophy where reading is concerned, the most frequently heard question is, "How and where do I begin to teach the deficient learner?" Educators must learn to use all available materials and adapt them as necessary to the needs of the children who exhibit various disabilities.

The purpose of this section is to explore some specific patterns or techniques for teaching that can be utilized and adapted to most of the available basic reading series or reading programs. The primary emphasis will be on instructional approaches to reading.

A Suggested Strategy for Teaching

An approach to teaching reading to students with learning problems can be expressed in the following design:
DEFICIT AMELIORATION + SIMULTANEOUS INSTRUCTION =
INTEGRATIVE LEARNING
Although one objective of the educational plan or strategy for teaching is to raise the level of the deficit areas, teaching to the deficits alone does not insure integration with all other areas of learning. Therefore, initial teaching or remediation at the reading task level should begin utilizing the child's strengths, permitting him initial success and satisfaction in learning.

Simultaneously, on the other hand, the teacher must include work in the areas of weaknesses. Time spent utilizing and developing strengths helps the child to gain a positive attitude and may result in an increased interest in the reading task. It then becomes easier to work with him on his weaknesses especially when attempting initial reading instruction. This is true for children for whom failure has become the mode. The unfolding of problem areas through diagnostic teaching is accomplished by moving the learner through a structured process of assessment to determine the areas of breakdown.

Presently, many teachers feel that they must teach fifty to one hundred sight vocabulary words before beginning work on phonics or analytical skills. They fail to consider that the child with one or more deficits in the visual channel area, for example, may not be able to recognize, remember, or synthesize meaningfully what is presented to him visually. The effect of this disability may be an inability to learn by the sight word approach, and a child with this problem may find it difficult to learn even ten words as unique wholes. Reading instruction for this child should begin with the presentation of short visual units which can be blended into words using a basic phonic approach along with simultaneous training in his deficit (visual) areas. This approach to instruction helps him develop a needed sight vocabulary (associating sight with sound). The emphasis for instructional purposes is placed on a sound–memory or sound-to-sight approach.

On the other hand, a teacher may get a student who exhibits auditory channel difficulties in one or more of the areas of perception, imagery, or language. The reading instruction

Reading: Initial and Remedial Approaches

for this student should begin with a whole-word approach providing the student can blend sounds. Many teachers using a basal-reading approach require that the student learn all the letter names and sounds prior to formal instruction. The student with auditory problems may find it difficult or even impossible to learn to read with this approach.

The basic concepts to keep in mind when planning a reading program are

1. What is the best input channel or the open channel best utilized by the student to learn, i.e., visual or auditory (sequence of input)?
2. How much input can he take before breaking down or "jamming" (amount of input)?
3. How fast can he be taught before he breaks down (rate of input)?
4. When is the best time of day to teach him and for how long, i.e., short bursts or long sessions (optimal-teaching moment)?

Suggested Approaches

While the child with visual channel deficits finds it difficult to learn whole words as he may not be able to retain a visual configuration, the child with auditory channel deficits usually finds this the easiest way to learn. Such a child, even though he cannot associate a phoneme with a grapheme, can remember a visual sequence. There is evidence that supports the contention that auditory channel deficits are more debilitating than visual channel disabilities, especially with regard to reading (Golden and Steiner 1969).

In planning for the various disabilities, it is necessary for the teacher to find a book series that can be adapted to the needs of the different children. While any basal-reading series can be adapted to the needs of children with reading disabilities, the authors of this volume have found the linguistic series to be most appropriate for children exhibiting processing disorders.

Certain of the linguistic series have much to offer children with learning difficulties. Linguistic books, however, have certain strengths and weaknesses. If used according to the specified instructions of the authors, it becomes evident that the child with the auditory channel deficit (with the visual channel intact) will find it an easier way to learn to read while the child with visual channel deficits may find it a more difficult way to learn since he cannot retain a configuration or a whole word.

Some linguistic approaches, however, lend themselves more to teaching children whether their deficits are visual or auditory in nature or even if the child is deficient in both areas. With just slight variations in the initial teaching approach, children with different problems can be in the same series of readers but on quite different individualized programs.

In applying such a broad rehabilitative program the first step a teacher would take would be to analyze systematically the selected reader. Since poor readers as a group have been traumatized by books, it is important that the book itself is not used initially. The book is introduced when the child can read it and is not used to teach him to read.

Where to Begin in Initial Teaching

The first step is for the teacher to analyze the series he intends to use:

1. List the words he finds.

CHAP. 6   Task Level Curriculum

2. Note the spelling patterns these words follow.
3. See how rapidly the vocabulary is expanded.
4. Note the sight words and how fast they are introduced.

The second step is to analyze the introduction of letters of the alphabet.

1. Note what phonetic elements are to be taught and in what order.
2. Note the introduction of letters with similar auditory and/or visual discriminations. How have they been spaced? By spaced, we mean how and where have they been introduced in the reader. Are they spaced far enough apart to avoid unnecessary confusion for the child with an auditory or visual disability, for example,

> *t* and *d* spaced (aural)
> *t* and *f* spaced (visual)
> *p* and *b* spaced (aural and visual)

Note: In initial teaching, the teacher should always select letters that do not look alike or sound alike. For best results, he should avoid teaching: *Sound alikes*, such as *p,b; k,g; t,v; sh, ch; Look alikes*, such as *b,d; f,t; m,n; Letters that can be inverted,* such as *m,w,* or *u,n* together.

Analysis of Sample Linguistic Readers

Two different linguistic approaches can be seen in the following examples.

EXAMPLE A: The teacher begins with the teaching of the long vowel sound "o" followed by the spelling pattern "op." The child is not taught that "o" has different sounds but only that the "o" in "no" says "o" and that the spelling pattern "op" says "op." The intent is that spelling patterns should be taught through a simultaneous blending of the auditory and visual components. The rules that govern accentuation and syllabication are not taught at this time, but this is actually the child's beginning training in open and closed syllables.

EXAMPLE B: The teacher starts with only short vowel sounds teaching the spelling patterns "an," "at," etc. These spelling patterns can also be taught through a simultaneous blending of the auditory and visual components.

FIGURE 6.1   Example A.

Word list	Page no.	Spelling patterns	Sight words	New letters used
go, no	1	Long "o"	——	g, n
a	3	——	a	——
yes	4	——	yes	——
hop, mop	7	op	——	h, m
fog, log	11	og	——	f, l
I, me, he	15	Long "e"	I	——
she	17	Long "e"	——	sh
and	18	——	and	——
we	20	Long "e"	——	w
hen, ten	24	en	——	t

Reading: Initial and Remedial Approaches

FIGURE 6.2   Example B.

Word list	Page no.	Spelling patterns	Sight words	New letters used
pan, man	1	an	————	p, m
a	2	————	a	————
ran	3	an	————	r
an	5	an	————	————
the	6	————	the	————
rat, fat	9	at	————	f
cat, see	11	at	see	c
I	12	————	I	————
can	14	an	————	————
sat	16	at	————	s

After analyzing the sequence of steps in each of the two examples, the teacher should be able to develop a teaching plan based on both the disabilities of the student and his intact learning channels.

Let us first look at the student with a visual channel deficit and the types of problems he might experience in learning to read. (This would be a good time to review the chapters that refer to visual channel deficits).

Visual Channel Deficits

Learners with visual channel disorders cannot as a rule retain the visual image of a whole word and need a more elemental or analytical approach to reading. If the student can blend sounds, the recommended method is one that teaches isolated sounds that can be blended into meaningful words. The basic approach is initially phonic oriented.

Note: The learners must have adequate auditory closure (blending) for this approach.

EDUCATIONAL PROCEDURES:

1. Consonant sounds should be taught first.
2. The teacher should look at the analysis of the series to be used—if an Example A type series is used, teaching would begin with the consonants "n" and "g"; if an Example B type series is used, teaching would begin with the consonants "m" and "p."

It is important that the initial consonants that are presented to the student be different in both appearance and sound. Students with visual discrimination difficulties tend to confuse letters which appear similar. They may also fail to note internal detail (log for leg) and have difficulty recognizing or remembering the different configurations of such words as *ship* and *snip*. Some exhibit inversion tendencies such as misreading "m" for "w" and "u" for "n."

The first step in teaching consonant sounds is to print the letters on 3 by 5 inch white cards in the presence of the student, preferably next to him or from behind the student so he

CHAP. 6 Task Level Curriculum

can see you produce it in the correct position. The letters should not be reproduced while the teacher is facing the student as the child will be getting a reversed image. All printing should be as consistent as possible, done in heavy black ink and in lower-case letters. At this stage, the teacher should begin by teaching the letter sounds only. It is usually best, initially, not to teach letter sounds in association with a key word such as "b" for "boy" as this may confuse the child.

The teacher should begin with a letter sound that cannot be distorted regardless of how long it is held such as "m" or "n." It is important that the consonant sound not be followed by a vowel sound verbally. For example, "t" should be said quickly and lightly, not drawn out into "tuh." If the sound is accented, for example, "puh" for "p," it may be difficult for the learner to learn to blend.

The second step is to hold the card up and say to the student, "This is 'm' (sound)." The child should repeat the sound with the teacher, then he should say it alone. The teacher should ask the child to think of other words that begin with the sound of "m." Classification type games can be introduced here for example, "I am thinking of an animal that starts with the sound 'm,'" or "How many things can you think of that start with 'm.'" After teaching the sounds of the two or three consonants the teacher has selected, the student should be given one flash card at first (later he will select the correct one from among others) and the teacher would say, "Show me the *m*," or "Give me the *m*." This type of activity helps the learner build a strong association between the visual symbol and the auditory referent.

If the learner has difficulty making the auditory–visual association, such as sounding letters, the teacher should introduce a tracing technique or use clay to form the letters. If a tracing technique is used, the child should trace his fingers over the letter while saying the sound, or the following tracing options can also be useful:

1. Tracing letters on paper using finger paint.
2. Forming the letters out of clay (let the child roll the clay into a snake and then form the letters).
3. Tracing letters in a box of damp sand.
4. Tracing letters that have been raised on paper. (A simple technique is to cut a piece of copper screening, 8 by 10 inches, and bind the edges with electrical or masking tape.) Using newsprint, the teacher places a sheet of paper over the screen, and then writes with a black crayon. The raised letter can then be easily traced with the finger.

As soon as the student learns a few consonants and one vowel he should be taught to blend these sounds into meaningful words. Nonsense syllables should not be used, and all words should be within the learner's spoken vocabulary. It is usually easier to begin with basal consonants and with words such as *an, man,* or *no.* As soon as the child is taught a word, he should be asked what it means and if possible, to demonstrate this with a motor response. He should then use it in a sentence.

In teaching blending, the letters can be placed on cards and then the cards can be physically pushed together.

Example one:

1. The learner is given a card with *o* on it, and he says "o." He is then given a card with an *n* on it. The two cards are then pushed together by the student while he says "n–o" and then "no." ([n][o])

Reading: Initial and Remedial Approaches

2. Plastic letters can be used in the same way. They should be lower case, however, and all of one color.
3. Clay letters, made by the child, can also be used in the same way. The *o* is placed on the table and the student moves the *n* beside it saying "n–o" and then "no."

Example two:

The letters *a* and *n* can be taught in the following manner:

1. The letters *a* and *n* can be presented together to form a word or taught as *an*, which is a spelling pattern. Cards that can be pushed together, plastic or wooden letters, or clay should be used.
2. When the *an* pattern is understood, the letter *m* can be introduced to the above pattern to form the word *man*. The student should be taught to say "an," and then as he moves the "m" over to say "man."

Once the first words have been taught, the learner should be allowed to mix the cards or plastic letters up and then re-form the word he was working on. In this way, he will experience analysis and synthesis. The teacher should always have him say the spelling pattern and then add the new letter. For instance, the learner would say "an" then move the *m* and say "man," or he would say "an" and then move the *p* over and say "pan." An associative clue such as a picture drawn on the back of the word card by the student will help him remember the word better.

The next step will aid the learner in developing his sight vocabulary. He should be able to see spelling patterns more readily if taught in the following manner:

1. The spelling patterns and words should be placed on 3 by 5 inch white cards and shown to the student while the teacher is saying the words in the following sequence:

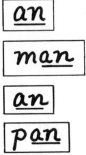

2. The teacher would say "an" (showing the "an" card) as in "man" (also showing the "man" card). Next, the teacher would show the "an" card and say, " 'an' as in 'pan' " (showing the "pan" card).

Note: Some time may elapse before Step 2 is completed as it takes some students longer to see these relationships.

3. When the teacher feels that the student has mastered these two tasks, he can then take away the cue card "an" leaving just the whole words "man" and "pan" and then ask the student to name the family and then the word. This may be quite difficult and require many repetitions, however, it is an important step in learning by this approach.

CHAP. 6 Task Level Curriculum

All of the teaching so far has been done without showing the learner the book. If the child was taught from Example Series A, for instance, he would know the words *go, no, a,* and *yes* before being introduced to the book. The mode inherent in this approach is success rather than failure. The sequence suggested in this approach can be called A V plus TK, if necessary (Auditory–Visual plus Tactile–Kinesthetic).

When success has been achieved with a few words, other word families can be introduced. These students cannot be expected to manipulate or revisualize the letters to form word families in their minds, therefore, they must be shown how the patterns are similar. They need something concrete to manipulate in order to see exactly how the words are formed and changed. It will take much deliberate teaching, repetitions and reinforcements before the child can be expected to see relationships between words.

Word families can be presented as members of a family living in a house together. The learner is encouraged to draw a house at the top of his paper and to put the letter e in the doorway. Other members of the family are then shown under the house. Care should be taken to line up the family being taught. The house of "e" would look like this:

Word families can also be presented with cards, raised screen letters, plastic letters, and clay. The word family can be brought to the child's attention further by having him put down the clay or plastic consonant letters and then sliding the single e down the line while he says the words. Another approach to this exercise would be to have the student put down three e's in a row, then place the *m, h,* and *sh* in front of the e's.

Reading: Initial and Remedial Approaches

If the student was taught from Example Series B, he would learn *pan, man, a, ran, an,* and *the* before being presented the book. The teacher must remember that the goal is "success," as we do not want to leave the child with a failure. Some teachers teach "just one more sound or word." This is how we "jam" the child, causing him to forget the other things that have been taught.

Sight Words

Sight words are taught in a way similar to that suggested for Example Series A by using clay, tracing, plastic, or wooden letters or cards. It is recommended that sight words such as *is, and, I,* etc., be taught as whole words first and in phrases or sentences. For example, *and* can be taught with *he, me,* and *she*. The teacher can pin cards with the words *me, she,* and *and* on students and arrange them so that they make short phrases, such as:

> he and she
> she and me
> she and he.

These phrases can be written on sentence strips and then cut up for the students to put back together. They can also be color coded on the back for self-correction.

Consonant digraphs should be taught as they are introduced in the reading series. For instance, in Example A, *sh* is introduced early. This is an isolated instance and so it is taught without a lot of explanation to the student. The sound "sh" is easily said without distortion and poses little, if any, problem despite the longer visual unit.

When introducing the student to two letter consonant blends, the student should be encouraged to think of both the sequence of the sounds and the form of the letters. The teacher should encourage him to think of the blends as a single unit but should keep him sounding out the letters individually until they are well established. For example, the *fl* in fled can be taught *f–l–e–d* initially. (Concrete materials should be used if needed.)

Terms like "long vowel" or "short vowel" sounds should not be used as they tend to confuse some children. Some students have great difficulty with learning and applying rules. The teacher should present vowel digraphs such as *oa* and *ay* with a simple explanation such as, "When you see these two letters together they usually say ____."

A good deal of spelling and writing is used in the sight-word approach. As soon as the learner is able, he is encouraged to transfer from his clay figures, plastic or wooden letters, or cards to his own written work. When teaching families, it is preferable to use lined paper cut into long strips, leaving room for the child to draw a house at the top and then to list the words in the family below.

CHAP. 6   Task Level Curriculum

After acquiring groups of basic sight words, the student should be encouraged to write short stories using these words. He can then cut pictures out to illustrate the stories and make his own collection. This will reinforce the learning and also increase the interest level.

Throughout the process, the child should always be encouraged to look for the like elements or spelling patterns within words. When he looks at a word, he should see letter groupings that represent auditory patterns. It is important to remember that when using the intact channel as the primary input for instruction that the areas of disability must be simultaneously ameliorated both during the initial teaching period and along with the remedial program. The discrepancy between strengths and weaknesses must not be allowed to widen, and hopefully a decrease will become apparent with proper training. Many good commercial, as well as homemade materials, are available for the amelioration or strengthening of deficits.

Auditory Channel Deficits

The learner with auditory channel deficits usually learns better through the whole-word or sight-word approach. He finds it difficult to relate symbols to their auditory counterparts and, therefore, cannot transfer the learning of sounds. These children usually must learn each new word as a unique entity as they cannot relate part of a word to a whole. They need to make a direct association between the symbol and the experience for each word.

EDUCATIONAL PROCEDURES:

1. The teacher should make sure the child understands the relationship between the written and spoken word. To help develop awareness of auditory–visual correspondence, the teacher can take a favorite book and point to the title. As he reads the title, he should point to each word with his finger. (To begin with, titles with one syllable words only should be used.) The child should be asked how many words he heard. The teacher would say the title and let him count with his fingers and then ask him how many words he sees. When the learner understands what the teacher is doing, he should point to each word as the teacher says it. The teacher should show the student other books and see if he can tell him how many words are in the title. Whenever possible, matching records and books should be used so that the student can listen to someone read a short sentence or story and follow along with his finger.
2. In selecting the child's beginning reading vocabulary, the teacher should make sure the words are within the student's range of experience and different with reference to sound and visual configuration. Nouns or pronouns that can be matched to associative clues such as pictures of objects should be used, with the teacher always making sure the student can pronounce all of the words.
3. The teacher should examine the analysis of the series to be used—if it is an Example A type series, teaching would begin with the whole words *go, no,* and *yes;* if it is an Example B type series, teaching would begin with the whole words, *pan, man, ran, a, an,* and *the.*

It is important to remember that one of the difficulties encountered with these students is teaching them discrimination of short vowel sounds. Many are unable to discriminate initial- or final-sound similarities or differences. Because of this, they cannot form generalizations that apply to new words and cannot break a word into syllables or individual sounds. Although the learner may know all of the sounds of the letters, he may be unable to blend them into words. The recommended procedure, therefore, is to work from the whole to the parts.

Teaching Sequence

The input sequence here is the whole word, then sounds, and then touch or Visual→Auditory plus Tactual–Kinesthetic, if necessary. When the teacher is sure the child can say the word and understand its meaning, he should concentrate on teaching him to match the word with a picture. It is not enough for the student to just listen and repeat the words, he must relate the word to a picture or other associative clues; otherwise, he will be merely going from the auditory (sound) to the visual (word) and may not be tying it in with meaning. Anna Gillingham, who contributed so much to our knowledge of reading problems in children, stated that, "The constant use of association of all of the following—how a letter or word looks, how it sounds, and how the speech organs feel when producing it must be stressed." (Gillingham and Stillman 1965)

If an Example A type series is used, the children in the reading group can play an integral part in illustrating the words. The children should always be involved actively. They can be given cards with the pronouns written on them; for example, a boy would be *he*, a girl *she* and two children could share a card and be called *we*. The children should be encouraged to make up sentences using the words. The word *and* can be added as indicated previously and they can stand, holding their cards and form themselves into phrases such as "*he and she*," "*she and he*," and "*she and I*," etc. If an Example B type series is used, pictures can be drawn on cards and used for matching with the printed word.

After thorough visual–auditory teaching, if the child is still unable to learn the words, he should then be introduced to a tactual–kinesthetic approach. Clay, tracing, and plastic or wooden letters are a few of the techniques that can be used.

In 1943, Grace Fernald said, "We find great individual differences in types of recall image." (Fernald 1943) She then went on to explain that for some children, seeing, hearing, and speaking must be reinforced with the concrete kinesthetic experience of handling and moving individual parts. Through the sense of touch, the student establishes a mental concept that is strong enough to support his memory retention. However, the authors of this volume feel that the *K* and *T* in the Visual–Kinesthetic–Tactual approach should not be automatically introduced. They should be introduced only after failure with the intact channel alone. Introducing the tactual automatically may overstimulate and, in fact, confuse some children.

After the child has learned his first basic sight vocabulary, word families can be presented exactly in the same manner as they were introduced to the child with the visual and kinesthetic channel deficit. Although it will take many more repetitions as each new spelling pattern is presented, this sequence of activities is necessary to help the child develop the ability to analyze and synthesize sounds. Most first grade phonics work is done orally and, therefore, is not appropriate for teaching these children. They need the simultaneous presentation of sound and visuals such as clay, plastic, or wooden letters, or cards. When the child has put his words into word families, the teacher should immediately ask him if he sees anything that is the same. He must then underline the spelling pattern that is being emphasized. (Visual reinforcement.) Next, the teacher should have the student say the words to see if he hears the identical elements (tying the auditory to the visual), i.e., "top," "hop." The emphasis here is on the development of an awareness of consistent configurations. The teacher should exaggerate the sound he wants the child to hear. The child must then exaggerate the sounds himself. The teacher should always use concrete materials that the student can manipulate so that he is continuously involved in doing as well as looking and listening.

Moveable letters are more effective when placed on a chalkboard or on a slanted surface so that the student can underline the pattern being emphasized with chalk:

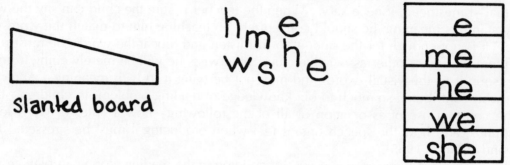

As the child starts to learn the basic vocabulary, the teacher must simultaneously work on improving his auditory skills to prevent difficulties later on with spelling. In severe cases, if the deficits are ignored, the auditory processing of data may become almost non-functional. These severe cases may need to be considered similar to educating deaf children. It should be noted that some tests of auditory discrimination do not always identify a child whose primary disability is perceiving sounds within words as, for example, the "and" in *hand*. A child's inability to do this often goes undetected for a long time. Teaching word families with concrete materials for manipulation and exaggerating the sound of letters and words the teacher is trying to teach will help the child with this type of problem. The teacher may have to go back to simple auditory-discrimination activities with varying input to include non-social, non-verbal sounds (tones of different pitch, frequency, and intensity), social non-verbal sounds (house and animal sounds), or social verbal sounds (letters and words) (Johnson and Myklebust 1967).

Some of the remedial activities should include using consonants that can be sustained such as *m, s, sh, v, r,* and *l*. The teacher would ask the child to say one sound and then he would say the others. The child should be told to stop the teacher when he says his sound. Children with this type of problem need to concentrate on the way in which the sound is formulated and the lips and tongue positioned. Mirrors can be used to help them see their mouth movements.

Some children know all of the sounds but are unable to blend them. It is easier to blend syllables than single consonant and vowel sounds. It should be noted that difficulties may develop later when the child starts to learn consonant blends such as "st" in *rust* and the "ft" in *left*. Unless the child is deliberately taught to notice and pronounce the words correctly, the "s" may be left out of *rust* and the "f" out of *left*.

It is very important that these children hear the number of syllables in a word. The teacher must instill a consciousness of both the number and the order of sounds within the word. He should always stress the rhythmic sequence of words, starting with one, then going to two, and finally, into three syllable words. Concrete materials for manipulation can be used effectively at this point. Only after the child is secure with the words and phrases he has learned should he be introduced to the book, especially if he has a long history of failure.

Auditory–Visual Channel Deficits

Golden, evaluated a group of children to determine possible differences in specific auditory and visual functions pertaining to good and poor readers of normal intelligence. (Golden and Steiner 1969) The results indicated that in this particular sample "poor" readers were lacking primarily in auditory rather than in visual skills. These authors conclude that "the significance of these auditory skills may have been overshadowed and eclipsed by the amount of visual material made available to the teacher."

Children with both auditory and visual channel problems, for example, should begin with the long vowel sounds first, as it is easier to discriminate between them than between the short vowel sounds. It is not enough, however, for these children to see, hear, and then say the word. Words must be matched with pictures or objects whenever possible and thoroughly reinforced with concrete material, such as clay, plastic, or wooden letters. Through the use of the tactual modality, the student will be able to feel and sense letters and words. This will also help the student to achieve closure (blending) and eventually remember better. The learning process may be slower, and it may be some time before the teacher can really ascertain whether transfer has taken place with the child who has multi-channel deficits. These children usually need extensive work to help them hear initial and final sound similarities and to discriminate between the short vowel sounds. They often have difficulty forming generalizations about new words and exhibit problems in syllabication and/or individual sounds. They are generally found to be unable to blend efficiently.

Tracing and writing are the manipulative aspects of reading that are a very necessary part of this program. The input sequence for this child is one that emphasizes seeing how a word looks, listening to how a word sounds, and noticing how it feels to say it by placing the child's hand on his own face and throat. The student should become aware of how the word feels when he writes it. This implies using the Visual–Auditory plus Tactual modalities simultaneously.

Summary

The techniques discussed in this section are designed to guide the teacher in breaking down the various available linguistic approaches. Most of these approaches have the same basic format, and all the teacher needs to do is to analyze the linguistic series in the same manner as illustrated in Examples A and B and then merely adjust the vocabulary in terms of rate, amount, and sequence of input as suggested for children exhibiting different learning problems.

A PERSONALIZED APPROACH TO READING

A modified experience approach to reading can be used for students who are beyond the initial stages in the elementary grades as well as for secondary and adult students. Many students have come to dislike books due to continued failure in reading over a period of years. Teachers have found that it is difficult to get the older student involved in reading by using a basal series which is far below his mental age or chronological age in terms of concepts and format. These books are often referred to as the "baby books," or "kid books," and secondary

CHAP. 6 Task Level Curriculum

age poor readers, as a group, are reluctant to use the primer through level-4, basal readers.

Alternative approaches have been introduced by teachers to include (1) linguistic series; (2) high interest, low vocabulary books; and (3) the experience method. Most of these techniques have built-in problems for the older child.

1. The vocabulary of the *high interest, low vocabulary books* in most cases, is too difficult for the student reading below grade level three.
2. *The experience approach* requires a strong visual–memory which, in many cases, is the very thing that prevents the student from learning in a basal series. Another factor is that motivation and interest are just not high enough to carry the student without good word attack skills. The student can hold just so much until his visual–memory fails him.
3. The *linguistic series* as a group appear to be too juvenile especially at the lower levels to many students. This approach as with the basals still requires the student to have a good visual–memory, even though the vocabulary unfolds at a slower pace. The illustrations in the linguistics or basals are often too juvenile even if the story is not. The interest level is often not appropriate for older students.

A Linguistic Based Experience Program

The following is a suggested modified experience method that incorporates a spelling pattern technique based on the linguistics approach to reading. This program is composed of four components plus a writing approach.

COMPONENT ONE—*Student's present sight vocabulary (what does the student have?).* The teacher or tester may report that the student has few words in his sight vocabulary as determined by standardized testing. Experience has shown that students who have been in school for a number of years who have anywhere near average intelligence have by merely attending school acquired a sight vocabulary. This sight vocabulary, however, may be comprised of words, many of which are not found on standardized tests, and therefore, not measured. The first step involves giving the student word lists, newspapers, books, etc., and having him circle or copy on paper the words he knows. After this is checked, he should list the words he knows separately on 3 by 5 inch white cards. When he has completed this task, the teacher should have him put an associative clue such as a picture or a short phrase using the word on the back of the card. Let the student hold the stack of cards so that he can see that he has a "reading vocabulary." Many of these students are convinced that they have almost nothing as far as reading is concerned and, therefore, develop a poor attitude toward books and, even more important, emotional barriers in terms of learning to read. Therefore, it is recommended that the student not receive a book until he can read it with 100% success. After the student has completed the stack of word cards he can read, he can then put them into a small file box. He should then be told that he is going to add many more to his collection.

COMPONENT TWO—*Student's interest (what does the student like?).* The teacher should develop a vocabulary made up of words dealing with an area of interest to the student. For example, if the student is interested in cars, the teacher can make up a list of words that con-

Modified Experience Approach to Reading

cern cars: make, type, parts, etc. The student and the teacher should build the list together. As the words are learned, they are placed on 3 by 5 inch white cards with associative clues on the back and then added to his word collection. These words will be introduced <u>one at a time</u> into the writing program.

COMPONENT THREE—*Spelling patterns.* The student is introduced to spelling patterns such as, *at, op,* and *an.* He learns these one at a time along with the sounds of four or five consonants, such as "p," "m," "t," and "g," if he does not already have them. He then blends the sounds (consonants and spelling patterns) together to make words. The words are also written on 3 by 5 inch white cards and filed with those he knows and with those he likes and has learned. The following is a list of spelling patterns and examples of combinations that can be derived therein. In teaching, the cards should be presented to the student like this: [m][an] and not like this: [m] [an]

a. *Consonant vowel–consonant* ([C] VC). This pattern should be taught first, for example,

 an — m an, c an, p an, t an
 at — c at, f at, s at, m at
 ap — c ap, t ap, n ap, m ap
 ed — w ed, b ed, l ed, T ed
 en — t en, p en, h en, B en

Other vowel consonant spelling patterns are:

 ab, ad, ag, am
 ed, eg, em, ep, et
 ib, id, ig, im, in, ip, it
 ob, od, of, om, on, op, ot
 ub, ud, ug, um, un, up, ut

The teacher should begin with the following consonants as they can be sustained without distortion for longer periods of time: *f, h, l, m, n, r, s,* and *v*. Then he should use such sounds as *b, g, t, d,* and *p*, and add the rest of the consonants as necessary. With the above consonant vowel sound combinations, many words can be formed. By using word cards or plastic or wooden letters, that the student physically pushes together and pulls apart, analysis and synthesis of words can be taught simultaneously. The same process is used with the patterns to follow. The student can be told this is a spelling program.
Note: Digraphs and blends are added to the pattern in the same way as the initial consonants. Again, if word cards are used, the letters should look like this; [ch][at] and *not* like this: [ch] [at]. For example,

 at — ch + at = *chat*
 at — th + at = *that*

Other digraphs and blends that can be used with spelling patterns are:

CHAP. 6   Task Level Curriculum

ch, cl, cr
dl, dr
fl, fr
gl, gr
pl, pr
sc, sh, sn, sm, sp, st
th, tr, tw
wh, wr

   b. *Consonant–vowel consonant (C V [C]).* This is an alternate approach if Section A does not prove successful, for example,

ba — ba *d*, ba *t*, ba *g*, ba *m*
ca — ca *t*, ca *b*, ca *p*, ca *n*
da — da *d*, da *m*, da *b*, Da *n*
fa — fa *d*, fa *n*, fa *t*, Fa *b*

Other consonant–vowel spelling patterns are:

ma, na, pa, ra, sa, ta, va, wa
be, de, fe, ge, je, le, me, ne, pe, re, te, ve, ye
bi, di, fi, hi, ji, ki, li, mi, ni, pi, ri, si, ti,
vi, wi, yi
bo, co, do, fo, go, ho, jo, lo, mo, no, po, ro, so, to
bu, cu, du, fu, gu, ju, lu, mu, nu, pu, ru, su, tu, yu

By adding the consonants *f*, *h*, *l*, *m*, *n*, *r*, *s*, and *v* as before, and then *b*, *g*, *d*, and *p*, many word combinations can be formed. Other consonants are added as necessary.

   c. *Consonant vowel–consonant–consonant ([C] VCC).* This pattern is taught next in the sequence, for example,

ash — *b* ash, *c* ash, *m* ash, *s* ash
ath — *b* ath, *m* ath, *p* ath, *r* ath
ang — *b* ang, *h* ang, *s* ang, *g* ang

Other vowel–consonant consonant patterns are:

esh, ish, ush
ath, eth, ith, oth
ing, ong, ung
ack, eck, ick, ock, uck
aff, eff, iff, uff
all, ell, ill, oll, ull
ess, iss, oss, uss

A Personalized Approach to Reading

> est, ist, ost, ust
> ask, esk, isk, usk
> asp, isp, osp, usp

Consonant blends and digraphs can be added as necessary to build many words.

    d. Consonant vowel–consonant–vowel ([C] VCV). This is the next phase in teaching spelling patterns, for example,

> ike — l ike, m ike, h ike, t ike
> ake — m ake, t ake, b ake, f ake

Other vowel consonant vowel patterns are:

> abe, ade, age, ame, ane, ape, ate
> ede, ete
> ibe, ide, ime, ine, ipe, ite
> ode, ome, one, ope, ote
> ube, ume, une, upe, ute

By adding the consonants mentioned previously as needed, many new words can be added to the student's list and put on 3 by 5 inch white cards with associative pictures or phrases on the back and filed. Digraphs and blends can also be added to the above vowel consonant– consonant patterns to make words. For example,

> ich — wh + ich = which
> ush — sh + ush = shush
> ing — br + ing = bring
>   th + ing = thing
> ong — th + ong = thong

    e. Other spelling patterns. Consonant digraphs and blends can be added to the following patterns to make the words:

eel	ead	oad	all	atch	athe
eed	eak	oak	ain	etch	ethe
eek	eam	oan	iad	itch	ithe
een	ean	oat	ose	otch	othe
eep	eal		oum	utch	uthe
eet	eap		use		
ange	aste	anch	aint	lege	
enge	este	ench	aize	ight	
inge	iste	inch	aise	ount	
onge	oste	onch	ease		
unge	uste	unch	east		

123

CHAP. 6 Task Level Curriculum

COMPONENT FOUR. An integral part of this program is the systematic introduction of words that are most common in everyday use. The Mann-Suiter Everyday Word List (Figure 6.3) can be used for this purpose. These words should also be introduced one at a time. As the student learns each word, it is written on a 3 by 5 inch white card with an associative picture clue or phrase on the back and is put in his file box. These words are introduced in phrases or sentences and not in isolation.

Coordinating the Components:

```
              What he has
             /          \
  What he likes      Spelling Pattern
             \          /
           Everyday Word List
```

Sample Lesson:

STEP I: *Learning a spelling pattern.*
Before introducing any new spelling patterns, the teacher should determine the learning strengths and weaknesses of the student. For students with auditory-channel problems, the words should be presented as whole words first, then broken down into consonants, digraphs, or blends and patterns. The student will need to see the same spelling patterns in the words. The sequence of teaching is as follows:

    First: cat — whole word shown on a card or with anagrams
    Second: c at — word broken down into sound and pattern on cards or anagrams.
    Third: cat — whole word shown on a card or with anagrams.

Note: Physical manipulation of cards or letters is important for students who cannot remember the patterns. The next step is to line up the letters and words as follows so the student can see the similarities.

```
(a.)   at         at      at      (b.)  c
       cat      c at      cat            m \
       mat      m at      mat            p — at
       pat      p at      pat            f /
       fat      f at      fat
```

Next, the teacher can mix up the letters and let the student build the words: *at, cat, mat,* and *pat*. The student then writes them on 3 by 5 inch white cards with pictures or phrase clues on the back and files them in his word box.

Note: The student should be tested the next day informally at his seat by the teacher showing him the words on cards and asking him to identify them. If he cannot identify them, the teacher should repeat the process but, this time, let him work for a longer period of time with the cards or plastic or wooden letters.

    For students with visual-channel problems, the initial steps would be different. The sequence for teaching this student is as follows:

A Personalized Approach to Reading

    First: c at   —   word broken down into sound and pattern on cards
    Second: cat   —   whole word
    Third: c at   —   word broken down again into sound and pattern (same as the first).
    Fourth: cat   —   leave the learner with a completed model

All of the other steps in teaching are the same as for the student with an auditory-channel problem.

STEP II: Now that the student has learned three words based on spelling patterns, he can incorporate them into functional use with the words he knows, words he likes, and everyday words by utilizing a:

Write–read approach

a. The teacher and student select out of all the words the student knows the ones he needs in order to write a sentence, paragraph, or short story. *Words he knows (selected by student from file cards)*
the, is, a, red, he, she, and, has, car, his, have, for

b. *Mann-Suiter Everyday Word List* [(Figure 6.3) *introduced one at a time and only taught in a phrase or sentence*] with

c. *words he likes (those the student chooses one at a time and which are only taught in a phrase or sentence)*
hot rod

d. *Spelling pattern (words he has learned)*
cat, mat, pat, fat

Paragraph writing can be accomplished in three ways:

a. The teacher can write the first sentence and the student writes the next one or vice versa, for example,

    Teacher: "Pat is a fat cat."
    Student: "The fat cat has a hot rod."

b. The student can write two sentences and the teacher writes the last one or vice versa, for example,

    Student: "The cat is fat."
    Student: "He is with Pat in the hot rod."
    Teacher: "The red hot rod has a mat for the cat."

c. The student writes a whole paragraph based on the above vocabulary, for example (sample paragraph),

    He has a hot rod. He is with Pat in his red car.
    Mat and Pat have the fat cat in the red car.

Each pattern should be developed into sentences, paragraphs, and then stories. In essence, the student is slowly developing a sight vocabulary. (Note: only one new thing is introduced at a time.)

CHAP. 6   Task Level Curriculum

Along with words, the student and teacher should be developing short phrase and sentence cards for quick sight identification. These should have associative picture clues on the back whenever possible. The Mann-Suiter Developmental Phrase List (Figure 6.4) can be tape-recorded for use by the student. There are many verbal feedback (recording) devices on the market which can be used with this program.

The student will soon build up many words based on patterns and gain confidence in himself. The teacher should remember that this student should not get any books to read until he can read them. After the student has built up a sight word vocabulary of approximately 200 words, he may be read to go into some of the high interest, low vocabulary books. The teacher must analyze the vocabulary in these books and incorporate words that the student does not know into the writing program. This is done before the book is given to the student to read. It is important to remember that the teacher must strive for success so that when the book is given to the student and he is told he can read it, the teacher can be sure that he is able to do just that.

SPELLING

Spelling is a skill that must be taught specifically. If differs from reading in that it demands complete recall of the words to be spelled. Skill in reading does not necessarily assure skill in spelling, but it is axiomatic that most poor readers are also poor spellers.

In order to spell fluently, a child must have:

1. A basic spelling vocabulary learned to the automatic level.
2. Ability to apply spelling generalizations to unknown words.
3. Knowledge of the meaning of the word to be spelled (ate, eight).
4. A "unique way" or method he can use to learn new words using his stronger "channel" for learning.

Areas of inadequacy that affect spelling are:

1. *Speech*—faulty speech patterns, dialects, and careless speech such as using "gonna" for "going."
2. *Auditory channel*—discrimination, or memory-sequencing problems.
3. *Visual channel*—discrimination, or memory-sequencing problems.

Regardless of any other problem, it is imperative that good study skills, study habits, and motivation through success and interest be included in any spelling program if it is to be successful.

At the turn of the century, spelling was taught by rote memorization. The assumption was that each word required a separate act of learning. Today, it is felt that a child should be helped to develop certain strategies for spelling, i.e., patterns in words such as the "and" in *sand* and *hand*. He should be taught to apply these spelling patterns instead of having to utilize a different strategy for each word learned. This takes advantage of the associative proc-

FIGURE 6.3 Mann-Suiter Everyday Word List.

a	here	the
all		to
am	I	they
an	in	this
and	is	three
any	it	ten
are	if	tell
at		two
	jump	talk
be		then
been	know	that
big		
blue	look	too
by	like	them
	little	there
can	let	
carry		up
come	may	
could	many	very
	me	
did	my	want
do	met	way
does		why
done	no	who
down	not	with
		was
eight	one	will
	once	would
for	on	what
four	of	where
		when
get	play	walk
go	pretty	went
gone		
good	run	you
got	ride	yes
going	red	your
green		yellow
	see	
hop	some	
had	so	
have	said	
he	saw	
	she	

CHAP. 6 Task Level Curriculum

FIGURE 6.4 Mann-Suiter Developmental Phrases.

I

it is	I hear a	I like a	a game
a big hat	did he miss	the pony is	we will walk
I see	we went to the	he rides a	her father
I took	I like my	I said	a pretty doll
in a hat	my name is	in the boat	a new book
the cat is	I live at	at school	the children
I had fun	my eyes are	I found	to the farm
I cut	he took me	a dime	a black horse
the cup	the room is	his work	a white rabbit
the bus	the kitten is	he has fun	the little boy
look at the	she is	at the farm	we will walk
I fed the	I wish I	he helped	they were
a cat is		is one	a little baby
I pet the	*II*	is pleased	a white duck
did he have		with me	a blue coat
he can	the ball is	the train	when you come
she will get	a chicken is	come in	to the tree
do you see	I took that	a ball game	you will like
he has a	my father is	he looks	a small boat
I want a	my mother is	to a game	a pretty girl
the band is	they are both	the baby	he would try
I like that	he drove a	the cat had	down the street
it was a	father drove	the cows are	a yellow hat
I saw	this is my	he was	went down
I can find	she saw the	he let	up the hill
I will	where are my	his horse	the brown horse
I play a	I put them		a big house
he sings a	here they are	*III*	a red bird
I want to	dad and I		in the garden
I kick the	the cow is	we like	into the water
she took the	the house is	after school	the little chickens
he likes to	the boy has	it snowed	my father knows
we got the	a horse is	some stories	he would go
he got a	there are	ask me	some cake
she got five	can you see	two trees	in the grass
he will ride	is there a	I am having	to the barn
I found his	I saw three	who worked	may I
can you	there were	with them	I must try
do you	one boy	would you	on the chair
I will give	two girls	your room	a baby pig
do you want	is a car	we went	some brown cows
dad got a	he knows	we can play	

esses and stabilizes the patterns of spelling in the child's mind. Eventually, this method must be converted as much as possible into more or less reflexive behavior.

Skills Needed before Starting a Spelling Program

A child should have certain basic skills before beginning a spelling program. Too often, poor spelling is the result of inappropriate methods imposed upon the child in attempting to teach him to spell. In teaching spelling, the teacher should make sure the child is able to discriminate sounds and articulate English speech sounds. Cultural and/or speech deviations should be noted, and the teacher should be realistic in his expectation for rapid change in this area. The student should also be able to discriminate visually between letters and be able to write upper and lower case letters of the alphabet. He needs sufficient strength and control of the fine muscles of the hand and arm in order to control and manipulate a writing instrument if a writing-to-reading-and-spelling approach is being used.

Auditory and visual memory-sequencing and closure skills are possibly the most crucial to spelling ability. In order to learn to spell fluently, a child must be able to remember sounds of letters in isolation as well as how to blend them into whole words. Once the child's phoneme-grapheme relationship becomes consistent, he will be able to use the skills of:

1. *Auditory-analysis*—to hear a word as a whole and analyze it into separate sound units.
2. *Auditory-synthesis*—to hear separate speech sounds and blend them into a whole word.

After the skills of auditory analysis and synthesis have been mastered, visual memory helps the child select the "c" for spelling *cat* rather than "k." Later, he may learn the rule that the "c" sound is usually spelled as a "k" when followed by "i" or "e," and that the word "kangaroo" does not follow the rule because it is a foreign word. Spelling rules are difficult for students with memory problems to remember. The student needs a great deal of practice using words functionally as in writing before the words can be revisualized. If a child in a spelling program is still visually and/or auditorially confusing *b*, or *d*, or *m*, and *w*, he may have difficulty moving from sheer rote memory to seeing the consistent language patterns that do exist in the English language. He should eventually hear and see that the "and" in *hand* is the same "and" in *sand* without having to learn each word separately.

The goal of spelling is to help the child develop as automatic a motor response as possible to the words he hears or visualizes in his mind's eye. This is a very different task from a spelling test in that there are no external clues, such as using the word in a sentence; and the child must reauditorize the sequence of the sounds in his mind.

Recognizing a word in reading does not mean that the student has noticed it in sufficient detail to spell it correctly. The child needs to develop a distinct image of the word so that he can recall it at will. Because great differences are found in individual recall, we find that some people get only very vague images, or none at all, and actually remember things in terms of audio-images, recalling the word with sound (through lip and throat movements), or even with the movement of the hand in writing the word. Other people with good visual memories remember words by actually revisualizing the letters.

One of the prerequisites to good spelling is a distinct and accurate perception of a word and the ability to describe it in detail. The child with a learning difficulty must be

CHAP. 6   Task Level Curriculum

taught through meaningful repetition until the process becomes so automatic that it can be written without conscious attention to the details of its spelling.

Each child will develop his own unique way to learn, and if he is ever to move from the realm of rote memory or memorizing each word as a single entity, he must be aware of both the systematic order in the structure of our language and his own learning style. Any spelling program then should take into consideration the manner in which each child learns in order to teach the basic principles needed for transfer of knowledge of one word to another.

Developing a Spelling Program

Aside from knowledge of how each child learns best, a teacher must have a spelling program that avoids introducing too many different vowel sounds at one time. It should be a simple program starting with letters and letter groups that most consistently represent the sounds of language.

Most commercial spelling programs are not applicable to children with learning problems because they are usually based on sets of words grouped around subjects. Little consideration is given to being consistent in the way words are presented.

Spelling programs could very easily follow the linguistic reading series presently available. By developing a language-spelling program around the reading series used, the teacher would be consistently using the same vowel sounds through writing, spelling, and reading activities. This would avoid use of the biggest problem most first graders face, which is "vowel cluttering." Occasionally, a child is unable to develop this cognitive processing ability. This is found when too many different sounds of the same vowel are presented close together causing vowel cluttering. (The "a" in *man* in the reading lesson becomes confused with the "a" in *Jane* on the same page and the "a" in *all* in the spelling lesson). Reading should be reinforced through a motor response such as building words out of letters, which is also spelling.

With simple variations, most linguistic reading series follow a prescribed order of presentation of words and can be an excellent outline for a spelling program. Most learners are ready for formal spelling when they have finished their first pre-primers and can read simple CVC (consonant–vowel–consonant) pattern words without hesitation.

The following spelling program outline is recommended for first-level readers:

1. The teacher should first introduce words of a simple *CVC* pattern (consonant–vowel–consonant). These could be analyzed and then put together using cards, or plastic or wooden letters.
2. Short vowel sounds should never be taught alone but always with a consonant, i.e., c at. The first spelling lesson could look like this:
   a. Family to be taught: *at*
   b. Select five words (start with nouns if possible): *cat, bat, hat, mat, rat.*
   c. Include a simple sight word that can be used with the nouns in simple phrases: *a.*

Note: The teacher should not try to teach all *at* words at one time.

The second spelling lesson would be another short "a" family such as "ad" with the words, *lad, mad, sad,* and *had,* and the sight words *I* and *see.*

Spelling

Note: The teacher should remain at each level until absolute mastery is attained. It is very important to overteach at this level to insure that the child has made these basic sound–symbol relationships.

In teaching lesson two, the teacher should reach back into lesson one and continue to use the words in phrases. He should introduce one short vowel sound at a time with from 3–5 words a lesson plus one sight word. After the short vowels have been mastered at this level, the child is ready to be moved on. The teacher should introduce:

1. Words of a simple *CVCC* pattern, using short vowel sounds ending with a double "ff," "ll," "zz," or "ss," for example, *tiff, tell, buzz,* and *kiss.*
2. Words having two letter blends with short vowels such as *plan, blot, chat, bring,* and *clap.*
3. Digraphs with short vowels (*ch, th, sh, wh*), such as *chat, that, shop, shut, when,* etc., continuing as suggested.
4. Three letter blends with short vowels such as *string, spring,* and *strap.*
5. Long vowels—words taught in group one with an added "e" such as *cap—cape; hat—hate; mat—mate,* etc.
6. Long vowels with two letter blends such as *spade* or *stove.*
7. Long vowels with digraphs such as *shade* or *while.*
8. Long vowels with three letter blends such as *stroke* or *strike.*
9. Second sounds of "c," "g," and "s," such as *city, garage, was.*
10. "R" controlled vowels, such as *ar, er, ir, or, ur.*
11. Vowel digraphs such as "ee" in *teen,* or "ea" in *bread,* or "ay" in *play.*
12. Silent letters such as "honest," "listen," or "knee."
13. Highly irregular words—impossible to decode—such as *said, the,* or *was*
14. Root (base) words and affixes such as *re, de,* or *bi.*
15. Words on the syntactic level of language such as bear—bare; or two—too—to.

In teaching spelling, the teacher should always try to move from one known element to the new or unknown element, adding to the sound–symbol pattern already known.

How Does Each Child Learn Best?

Before teaching spelling, a teacher needs to find out which combination of input produces the best output. The spelling suggestions given by textbooks are not suited to all children, and it is up to the teacher to help children understand that they do have an individualized method of learning how to spell.

Children who have difficulty in learning to spell should be taught spelling through their strongest "channel." Sometimes children having trouble with spelling hide their spelling errors behind a facade of illegible handwriting.

Visual Channel Problems

Children with visual, memory sequencing problems may learn best through an auditory, or sound spelling approach. The following is suggested:

131

CHAP. 6   Task Level Curriculum

1. In this method, the word is said by the teacher, spelled, and then said again. Next, the child says the word and spells it. The teacher repeats the process and then the child repeats it two or three more times before writing from memory.
2. Some children need a slightly different approach from the above. The teacher says the word, spells it, and then says it again. The child then writes the word and the teacher corrects it. The child writes it two or three more times and finally turns the paper over and writes it again.

Auditory Channel Problems

Children with auditory memory sequencing problems may learn best through a more visual approach. The following is suggested:

1. In this technique, a child is shown the word on a card or list and given the name. The child looks at the word, says it, spells it, and says it again. The word is removed and the child spells it from memory. After spelling it two or three times more, he then writes it from memory and checks the word against the stimulus card.
2. Some children need a slightly different approach from the above. The teacher shows the word and names it. The child looks at the word and then copies it on his paper. The word is then covered and the child writes from memory and then checks it two or three more times. After spelling it two or three times more, he then writes it from memory and then checks his word against the stimulus card.

Both Auditory and Visual Channel Problems

Children who have experienced problems with both auditory and visual, memory-sequencing need a multi-sensory approach. The following method is suggested: The teacher shows the word on a card, names the word, and spells it out orally. The child looks at the word, spells it, and then writes it on his paper. The teacher covers the word, and the child spells it orally from memory several times and then writes it from memory two times, turns the paper over, writes it from memory and checks it with the word card. Many repetitions may be necessary.

Note: Multi-sensory input is not always the best method for all children. The teacher should find the simplest approach that appears to be the most productive for each child.

Along with a visual–motor approach, the teacher should include a great deal of practice in listening, saying of words, and writing. Some of the manipulative material that can be utilized to reinforce spelling are:

1. Three by five inch white cards with associative picture clues on the back
2. Clay formed into letters
3. Plastic, wooden, felt, or beaded letters
4. Sand trays
5. Fingerpaint
6. Magnetic letters or a typewriter for older students

HANDWRITING

Difficulties in handwriting fall into two main categories: (1) factors that are more student based and (2) factors arising from an inadequate instructional program.

1. *Student-based difficulties:*
   a. Lack of readiness for beginning writing may be a factor in that the child may exhibit fine motor dysfunction of the hands and fingers or poor eye–hand coordination.
   b. The learner may have a visual acuity problem and need glasses.
   c. The child cannot grasp the pencil correctly or has an awkward writing position. He may have crippled hands or a spastic condition.
   d. The student may not have established a dominant hand. He may be switching from left to right.
   e. The learner may have difficulty retaining visual symbols rather than have poor visual–motor coordination.
   f. The student may have an emotional problem which can easily show up in a deteriorating handwriting. He could also be physically ill.
   g. The child may have no interest in writing and be unwilling to practice. He may exhibit indifference to established minimum standards.
2. *Program-based difficulties:*
   a. The child may have been started in a formal writing program before he was ready. Possibly he is still undecided as to which hand to use.
   b. There could be insufficient interest on the part of the student due to undifferentiated group drill. The wrong positioning of paper might be a factor.
   c. Not enough care taken with initial teaching may have been a factor, and the child was allowed to practice errors. Too much practice done without supervision can cause difficulties.
   d. A poorly planned transitional program from manuscript to cursive writing may be the cause of the problem in the older child.

Readiness for Handwriting

In the younger child, kindergarten through first grade, training should begin with indirect preparation for writing. Fine motor dysfunction is not uncommon in these children; therefore, there is a need for manipulative experiences designed to strengthen muscles needed for writing and pencil control.

TRAINING SEQUENCE. Activities that may help to develop fine motor skills necessary for writing are suggested below:

1. Manipulation of small objects is good such as knobs on puzzle parts, nuts and bolts, caps on small bottles, and cutting. Finger-painting, and clay modeling help to strengthen muscles for hand and finger control.
2. Geometric solid smooth wooden forms, △ ○ ▱, help the child to concentrate on

CHAP. 6 Task Level Curriculum

different shapes and to feel as well as to see the difference between a square and a triangle, for example.
3. Templates or metal insets #1 ◯ #2 ▢ will help perfect fine motor skills — hand and finger control. These can be used according to the following:
   a. The learner starts with frame #1 and traces around the inside first with his finger. He then traces two or three times with a soft colored pencil or plastic crayon.
   b. Then using a different colored pencil or crayon, the student fills in the center with short strokes │││↓ always made from top to bottom.

GRASPING OF PENCIL. Good writing starts with proper grasping of the pencil. If the child cannot hold the pencil correctly, the teacher should watch to see if he has trouble grasping other things. If he does have a problem the teacher can help him find a way to hold his pencil by using tape, rubber band, putting the pencil through a rubber ball, or by using any other aid. The teacher should be sure to place a note in the student's record indicating that he has taught the child an unorthodox method.

In teaching a child to hold a pencil, the teacher should always give directions through his strongest learning channel and try not to combine the *VAT* (Visual, Auditory, Tactual) all at once. He may be overloading him with too much input.

1. *If the child has a visual deficit,* he ought to be taught through the auditory channel. The child should be given clear oral directions as to how to hold a pencil. He may need to keep his eyes shut as he grasps the pencil.
2. *If the child has an auditory deficit,* the teacher should mark the pencil to show him where to hold it or else put some other "stop" in the proper place.
3. *If the child has an auditory–visual deficit,* The child should be asked to close his eyes and then, without talking, mold his hands around the pencil. The teacher should explain what he is going to do before he does it, and then explain again what he did afterwards. The teacher must not speak during the time he is molding the student's hands around the pencil.

Beginning Handwriting

In teaching a child how to write the training must be more direct and move from large scale, gross movements, to the necessary finer movements. This teaching process starts with

1. Large templates that can be used at the blackboard or on large sheets of paper (these help the child to feel as well as to see the differences between different geometric shapes)
2. Small templates which can be used at the desk
3. Scribble-scrabble on the blackboard, first with both hands and later with the dominant hand (for example, *eeee uuuu eee*)
4. Tracing over large printed letters, such as *a, b, c, d,* etc., on a plasticized sheet using a washable crayon or grease pencil
5. Writing letters in a tray of damp sand, or with a stick in a tray of soft clay
6. Writing with a pencil on paper.
Note: Be sure that the lines on the paper are clear.

Handwriting

Writing Must Have Meaning

As soon as possible, even at the readiness stage, writing should say something. Initially, the student needs to concentrate chiefly on learning the correct order of making the strokes. Right after this comes spacing. Whole words that have real meaning for the child and are easy to write are the best with which to start. Linguistic readers are well suited to this approach and will enable the child to begin writing that which he is already reading.

Until such time as the learner is able to write words from memory, he should have a copy or a model from which to write. The copy should be on the same kind of paper that the child uses although as the child improves he can copy phrases and sentences out of his reading book. Ten minutes at a time is usually enough writing for the younger children. Speed is never emphasized at this stage, and writing should always be supervised. Copywork from the chalkboard in the early stages that forces constant refocusing of the eyes should be avoided.

Manuscript Writing

Manuscript writing is based entirely upon circles and sticks, or lines. Before starting to teach, the teacher must consider the maturation level in terms of the previously mentioned skills of each of the students. Successful copying of circles is normative from about age 3. By first grade, it is important not only that a child can copy a circle but also how he produces it. By the age 5, most girls can make a circle from the top down in a counterclockwise direction. For most boys this is normative at 5½ years of age. After age 6, about 90% of both boys and girls start their circle from the top and go down in a counterclockwise direction. The one exception to this progression is the left-handed child. Lefties may be as old as nine years before a top to bottom counterclockwise circle is normative. The difficult part of making a circle is the return. The use of templates helps children to develop this ability.

Left-handed student's papers should always be turned so that the top points toward the right front corner of the desk. The students should also be taught to grip their pencils farther away from the writing point than is normal for a right-handed child and to keep their hand below that which they are writing. (This prevents smearing and they can see what they have written.)

Physical comfort must always be considered and so the seating of left-handed children in the classroom is important. They should be seated at the left side of the room facing the chalkboard in order to copy material from the board more easily. Some learners are slow in developing handedness. While dominant handedness is usually observable at the age of three, in some children it may not be fully developed until the age of eight.

Cursive Writing

Any program whether beginning or remedial should stress good letter formation. The letters causing the most trouble are:

        n that looks like an *m*

        a that looks like an *o*

a that looks like a *u*
a that looks like a *ci*
l that looks like an *i*
i not dotted that looks like an *e*
b that looks like an *li*
d that looks like a *cl*
t uncrossed and looped like an *l*

One very effective way to help a child achieve better letter formation is to use connected print script (see Figure 6.5). In *Language Skills in Elementary Education*, Paul Anderson gives detailed instructions on how this method can be used to help pupils in beginning cursive transition from manuscript to cursive writing. (Anderson 1964) This is also an excellent way of remediating a child who has developed poor writing habits.

Lower case letters should be introduced first in the following order:

l, a, d, t, u, n, m, h, k
w, e, b, v, x, y, j, f, s,
p, r, c, i, g, o, q, and z.

The letters *b, e, f, k, r, s*, and *z* must be taught specifically. Capital letters are always practiced in usage. The teacher should always use whole words in this approach and watch any word with an "n" in it as this requires different spacing. Another letter that can cause confusion is "g" as it changes with connections.

Transitional Writing

In teaching transitional writing the teacher should begin with the easier letters; he can add the difficult letters later one at a time:

1. First the word should be printed in manuscript.

all

2. Then a colored pencil should be used and the letters connected with a dotted line.

a.t.   *a.n.t.*

The child then traces over the printed manuscript letter and the connecting dotted lines to form the cursive writing. Difficult letters should be written lighter than the black dots and eventually fade out with successive tracings.

Handwriting

Note: Watch this problem with the letter *n*:

not pant pan

The "n" in the middle or end of a word must have enough room in front of it for the extra hump needed in cursive.

FIGURE 6.5

Easier (level one)								
a	c	i	o	u	q	t	u	w
a	*c*	*i*	*o*	*u*	*q*	*t*	*u*	*w*
Moderately Difficult (level two)								
e	d	g	h	j	l	m	n	p	y
e	*d*	*g*	*h*	*j*	*l*	*m*	*n*	*p*	*y*
More Difficult (level three)								
b	f	k	r	s	v	x	z	
b	*f*	*k*	*r*	*s*	*v*	*x*	*z*	

Remediation techniques for writing that deteriorates under pressure are as follows:

1. The child should be observed as he writes to see if he is doing it correctly. For instance, *i*, *j*, and *t* are dotted or crossed immediately in manuscript writing but not in cursive. Many children carry this habit over into cursive, and it slows them down.
2. If the learner is writing correctly but tires too easily, desk templates should be used to help him develop more strength in the muscles needed for writing.
3. The student who is an extremely slow writer should be watched. If he is slow because he can't read the material he is copying and has to copy each letter almost stroke by stroke, he may be a reading problem and not a writing problem.

Handwriting Screen

Visual–motor skills generally develop early in most children and tend to be sequential. Three primary problem areas are evident in children exhibiting handwriting difficulties:

1. Poor quality, or illegible
2. Acceptable quality but below minimum standards when pressured by the requirement of speed
3. Extremely slow rate but acceptable quality.

The teacher must identify early in the school year those pupils whose handwriting is illegible and of poor quality under normal daily conditions. Samples of the student's "best," "fastest," as well as "usual" handwriting can be used for diagnostic purposes. The teacher

CHAP. 6 Task Level Curriculum

should use materials that contain a vocabulary that is familiar to the child so he will have little difficulty with spelling or comprehension. He should include sentences that contain all the letters of the alphabet. A suggested sentence would be: "The quick brown fox jumps over the lazy dog."

1. *Usual sample.* A sample of the student's usual work should be taken under conditions that are not fatiguing.
2. *Best sample.* The teacher should say to the student, "Write the sample three times. Take your time and do your best. This is to be your very best effort." There should be no time limit.
3. *Fastest sample.* The teacher should say to the student, "Now I want to see how fast you can write. I am going to give you three minutes to write the sentence as many times as you can. I will tell you when to stop."

Now the teacher has a basis for comparing handwriting. Since reading and writing are interrelated activities, the teacher can utilize writing to reinforce reading.

The following should be considered in evaluating handwriting:

1. Can the student copy accurately?
2. Does the student align letters properly?
3. Does the student have an unorthodox joining of letters in cursive writing?
4. Does the student use neo-graphisms or squibbles that are not really letters?
5. Is there letter fusion such as writing *brick* for *brick*?
6. Does he use the same hand consistently for writing?
7. Does he write from left to right?
8. Does he have poor spacing of letters and words?
9. Are his letters of irregular size?
10. Does his work show fatigue? For example, his last line may be noticeably poorer than his first one.
11. Does he exhibit poor letter formation such as "*d*" like "*cl*", "a" like "*o*", "a" like "*u*", "t" like "*l*"?
12. Is he unable to recall or retrieve the motor act of writing as a form of expressive language?

Note: When an entire class is being evaluated, the teacher should note the time it takes for each student to complete the task. Some students can write well but take too much time. This is important diagnostically in terms of the amount of written material that is required of a particular student in a given time.

Handwriting for the Older Child

Children in the second grade and higher experiencing difficulty with either manuscript or cursive writing need a slightly different approach. In addition to collecting handwriting samples of the students above the following questions should be asked:

1. Was handedness changed at any time?

2. How much difficulty did the student experience with beginning writing or cursive if it is an older child?
3. Is the student extremely nervous or emotional? Has the handwriting become either much larger or much smaller?
4. What is the learner's general physical condition? Has he been ill or suffered a seizure?
5. What is his ability to draw, color, and cut?
6. Does the child have difficulty in some other basic subject such as spelling or reading?
7. Does he have a negative attitude toward some or all school work?

If the handwriting problem is actually rooted in reading and spelling problems, then just trying to remediate the handwriting problem by itself will not usually be successful.

As already indicated in the handwriting discussion on page 199, three kinds of difficulties in handwriting appear to emerge:

1. Poor quality, or illegible handwriting
2. Handwriting that deteriorates under pressure of speed. (By the fourth grade, speed is gradually encouraged.)
3. Handwriting that is produced at too slow a rate.

The overall objectives for good handwriting are legibility and ease of writing. The single most important factor in determining the legibility of handwriting is letter formation and then, to a lesser degree, spacing.

LANGUAGE

Suggested Teaching Strategies

The following is a description of how information can be presented to students in a developmental sequence. The following basic format for the presentation of information is applicable to all subject matter areas where language in terms of understanding and meaning is required. It is designed to aid the teacher in determining the best possible approach to structuring and controlling the language input in terms of the learning needs of individual learners. The following components should be considered in building good concept formation in children.

Level of Presentation

Concepts that lend themselves to physical representation can be taught using the following sequence of presentation.

1. *Concrete objects* or forms that can be manipulated by the students.
2. *Pictures* representing objects within the learner's experiences.
3. *Geometric shapes or forms*
4. *Symbols,* such as letters, numerals, and words, are the highest level of presentation.

CHAP. 6   Task Level Curriculum

Level of Conceptualization or Ideation

CONCRETE–FUNCTIONAL (C–F): Many concepts can be presented in any of the above mentioned forms to include objects, pictures, geometric shapes, or symbols. At a lower level of conceptualization, the language involving a particular concept can be defined as essentially descriptive or functional in nature, i.e., the word used tells us what it is, how it looks, what it is made of, what it does, and what it does not do, and what can be done with it. This level of language can be termed concrete–functional or the analysis of concepts in a concrete functional manner. An example of this level of conceptualization would be the following: The concept of elephant can be presented in concrete form, picture, shape, or word. It can also be described in concrete–functional terms such as "big," "heavy," and "it can carry people." Children who have language deficiencies should be introduced to concepts in terms of meaning by first being presented with the concrete form whenever possible. The language associated with the concept should be taught in a concrete–functional manner first.

ABSTRACT (A): The concept elephant, to continue the example, which can be presented in different ways (concrete form, picture, shape, or word) should then be examined in an abstract sense. The appropriate sequence in teaching the concept elephant, for example, is to first teach how it is different from other things. After difference is understood, teach how it is the same as other things. For example, an elephant is different from a horse in size, shape, behavior, etc. It is the same as a horse in that both have four legs, a mouth, two eyes, and are animals. The teacher can build in the meaning of the concept of elephant at different levels through teaching simple, then complex classifications and associations. This should be accomplished first visually by using visual associative clues such as a picture or object and then auditorily (through communication without the use of visual associative clues, such as objects or pictures).

Serendipity

The teacher should encourage students to look for relationships or functions that may at first appear to be unrelated but will, if properly combined, result in something unique or different. He should regard the following sequence in teaching:

1. Achieve good verbal behavior first which may entail beginning with single words, then short phrases, and finally sentences.
2. Introduce the concept through reading activities.
3. Reinforce through writing.

Note: All children do not need to manipulate the concrete object in order to achieve understanding. A great deal depends upon which level of presentation the child achieves the greatest amount of meaning and success.

Sample Lesson

The following is a sample language lesson dealing with the meaning of a specific concept that is within the child's range of experiences.

1. *Concept* — Ball.
2. *Level of Presentation* — object ball, picture of ball, shape of ball or the word ball, depending upon the presentation level best suited to the needs of the child.
3. *Levels of Conceptualization: Concrete – Functional* — What does a ball look like and feel like? What is it made of? What can you do with it? What can you not do with it?
4. *Abstract* — How is a ball different from a block, etc. How is it the same as a circle, globe, etc. (classification) What goes with ball, i.e., (simple association), ball is to circle as block is to ___? (Complex association).

Children need opportunities to experiment with words and express themselves freely in a non-threatening environment. The learner should be encouraged to express himself even if he does so in non-standard English. Constantly correcting the student's verbal expression often leads to the child inhibiting any spontaneous language that may have been forthcoming. Some teachers feel that disadvantaged learners as a group do not have good communicative language or are "non-verbal." Away from school, the language the child uses in most cases serves him well within his own social milieu. It may not, however, serve him in achieving success in what can be described as the language of school. This does not mean that children who appear to have a paucity of language in terms of standard English cannot "think" or be taught to "think better." The function of the teacher is to expand the experiences of the student as well as to aid the learner in expanding his own mind. This will come about by helping the student to derive greater meaning from experiences through the building in of good language acquisition skills.

ARITHMETIC

Arithmetic can be envisioned as another symbolic language as well as a means of indicating spatial–temporal relationships. A number sense is built early in the development of most children, as many of the concepts that deal with space, form, distance, order, and time are learned by the child through his everyday interactions with people, especially his parents, siblings, and peers. Mother helps formulate "math" concepts during feeding time when she says "a little bit more," or "just one more bite," etc. Problems in dealing with number concepts may result from language disorders, inability to deal with spatial–temporal relationships, and/or other specific processing deficits. Learning disabilities that affect reading, writing, and spelling tend to also affect arithmetic skills acquisition. No one basic task area can be considered in isolation in attempting to diagnose the problems of the learning handicapped child.

Visual Disorders in Arithmetic

1. The student may not be able to discriminate differences or similarities in size and shape (discrimination).

CHAP. 6 Task Level Curriculum

2. He may exhibit discrimination difficulties such as writing 3 for 8 or 2 for 5 (discrimination).
3. He may not be able to learn sets or groupings (closure or figure–ground).
4. The student may not be able to judge with accuracy spatial relationships that deal with distance and quantity (spatial).
5. He may have difficulty in learning to tell time (spatial–temporal).
6. The student may ruin materials, books, garments, etc., because he tries to force them into drawers or spaces that are too small. He may have difficulty in relating the size of an object to the appropriate container (spatial).
7. He may exhibit problems with the alignment and arrangement of numerals (spatial).
8. He may overpour his glass, have difficulty lining up buttons, and put too much food on his fork (spatial).
9. He may have problems with body image as indicated by the "Draw-A-Man" Test. (spatial–body image).
10. He may exhibit a poor sense of direction, getting lost easily, not being able to find different places in the school or neighborhood (spatial).
11. He may have difficulty with historical sequence and with geography that deals with maps and globes (spatial–temporal).
12. He may have problems with right–left orientation and placement (directionality in arithmetic).
13. He may have difficulty with relating himself to an object in space and appear awkward and clumsy in his attempt to perform a physical task (laterality).
14. He may have difficulty understanding cardinal and ordinal placement (memory-sequence, and/or spatial).
15. He may exhibit reversals and write Ɛ for 3, or inversions and write 6 for 9 (memory-sequence, and/or spatial).
16. He may not be able to write numerals (visual–motor).

Auditory Disorders in Arithmetic

1. He may not be able to retain an auditory sequence of numerals (memory-sequence).
2. He may have difficulty with looking at a series of numerals while counting aloud (memory-sequence and visual scanning).
3. He may exhibit difficulties with story problems which require him to assimilate and hold a great deal of information in his mind (memory-sequence).
4. He may not be able to cope with rapid oral drills (memory-sequence).
5. He may not be able to associate a numeral with its auditory referent (auditory-visual association).

Language Disorders in Arithmetic

Difficulties in receptive and expressive language that affect reading and writing will also affect the student's performance in arithmetic. The student may not be able to understand words that are associated with story problems. He may have difficulty with words or concepts that relate to space and time. This may include problems with understanding process signs and other vocabulary that includes words dealing with distance and measurement. Words such as "beside," "further," "in between," "within," "upside down," or "next to" may be difficult for the student to conceptualize. Words with a dual meaning such as "base," "times," "equals," etc., are difficult in that the student may not be able to shift in terms of the meaning of these words. He may not be able to retrieve numerals or words needed for arithmetical operations or be unable to express himself in terms of arithmetic in clear and sequential thought patterns.

Concept Teaching Sequence

It appears that number concepts need to be developed in a sequential manner. This consideration is particularly important when teaching children who have difficulties in the processing of information. In arithmetic, as in other areas of skill development, the level of presentation that appears to be most successful is the concrete one. This implies that the teacher must include a great deal of manipulative activities as part of the instructional program in each of the following developmental task areas:

1. VISUAL DISCRIMINATION (MATCHING):

Shape:

    a. Begin with small geometric solids and let the children feel and describe the differences and similarities between the various forms.
    b. Use form boards to include metal insets or templates to teach discrimination.
    c. Pairing off of objects and forms as used in a "Noah's Ark."
    d. Pictures or dittos of objects and geometric shapes can be used for matching purposes where the learner looks for differences as well as likenesses.

Size:

    a. Use insets or "nesting material" — cans that fit into cans, barrels that fit into barrels, or boxes that fit into boxes.
    b. Grouping by size of cylinders, blocks, etc., is good.
    c. Use different size rods or wooden dowels.
    d. Montessori material which can be used here includes, "The Pink Tower," "The Brown Staircase," and "Knobless Cylinders."
    e. Utilize pictures of geometric shapes and objects for size differentiation.
    f. Graded insets to include objects or geometric shapes can be used. For example:

2. GROUPING OR SETS

    a. Begin with "Hoola Hoops" and put objects inside.
    b. Use regular dominoes: ▢ ; then proceed to dominoes with sets: ▢
    c. Figure–ground activities should be used.
    d. Use matching sets of objects and forms printed on dittos. The learner will trace around identical objects or forms with the same color crayon.
    e. Tachistoscopic activities where the teacher exposes groups of dots for short periods is helpful. Begin with widely separated dots and gradually move the dots closer together. Blocks or coins can be used in the same manner.

CHAP. 6 Task Level Curriculum

3. VOCABULARY OF SPATIAL–TEMPORAL RELATIONSHIPS

   a. Obtain a concrete object such as a toy monkey and a box or some other container which can be used to teach concepts of space such as over, under, inside, outside, below, above, beside, next, near, alongside.
   b. The same thing can be taught using a toy squirrel and a cardboard tree.
   c. Concepts of time can be taught using stories or real experiences such as field trips that include such words as sooner, later, late, before, after, morning, afternoon, night, past, shortly afterward, almost, often, etc.
   d. Send the student on an errand and time him. How long did it take to get there? Did it take more time to get back? Was it a long or short trip?
   e. Parents can do a great deal of reinforcing activities at home that involve routine, day-to-day experiences as well as travel.

4. ESTIMATION

In all of the following activities, the student will be required to make judgment about spatial relationships without physically matching at first. After an estimation is made, he can then check for accuracy by manipulating the material or by other physical movements such as pacing off the distance.

Size:

   a. The student can estimate the size of other children in the class. Compare two children—"Who is shorter?" "Who is taller?" Then compare three or more children—"Who is the tallest?" "Who is the shortest?"
   b. Ask the student to compare objects in terms of larger and smaller.
   c. Place objects into various size piles and ask the student to rank them in terms of size.
   d. Use different size cards with their respective envelopes, and ask the student to estimate which card goes with which size envelope. Do not let him physically manipulate the materials at first. Later, he can check for accuracy.
   e. Give the student different size objects and different size containers, and let him estimate which object will fit into which container.
   f. Have the student physically compare different size rods, or dowels and rank them from smallest to largest.
   g. Ditto sheets can be used that require the student to compare the relative size of lines and geometric forms.

Weight:

   a. The student should hold and compare objects of different weights (begin with gross differences then go to finer differences).
   b. The student should be asked to make estimates as to the relative weights of objects without holding them. For example, "Which is heavier—a car or a bus?"
   c. Using different piles of similar objects, the student should rank them in terms of weight from lightest to heaviest.

Mann-Suiter Developmental Arithmetic Inventory

Shape:

    a. The student can estimate the fit of simple puzzle pieces.
    b. He can use form boxes to make judgments about shapes.
    c. Use ditto sheets which require the student to estimate shapes that interlock.

Distance:

    a. The student should estimate how many steps are required to go from one place to another (begin with short distances first).
    b. Have the student estimate how far he can throw a ball.
    c. Have him estimate the relative distance of objects to himself and from object to object in the classroom or outside of school. For example, "Which is closest to you — the tree or the fence?" "Which is further from the fence — the house or the telephone pole?"
    d. Have the student estimate the relative distance between a fixed point such as his home or his classroom and other geographic locations that are familiar to him.
    e. Use ditto sheets containing lines, geometric forms, or objects and have the student compare the relative distance of two or more objects from a fixed point such as a small dot in the middle of the page or from each other (begin with very simple comparisons).

5. COUNTING (ORAL)

    a. Begin by teaching rote counting from one to five through songs such as "One Little, Two Little, Three Little Indians", etc. (Later, count from one through ten.)
    b. Follow the counting songs with "Finger Plays." Begin with one to five and later count from one to ten.
    c. The students should do rote counting from one to ten.

6. COUNTING WITH MEANING (ONE-TO-ONE CORRESPONDENCE)

    a. Begin by asking the child to give each student in the class a piece of paper or some other item that needs to be distributed.
    b. Have the student fill a row of holes with pegs, beads, pebbles, or discs.
    c. A variation of number two would be the addition of a drum beat as the child performs each task.
    d. Play, "Tea Time" and have the student prepare settings of napkins, dishes, and utensils for a group of children who are already seated. A more advanced activity of this nature would be to prepare settings for a specific number of individuals who are not present.
    e. Use paper dolls, and have the student give each one a costume.
    f. Have the student match nuts and bolts and fit them together.
    g. Use 2 by 2 inch cardboard squares, and have the student put wooden, plastic, felt, or magnetic numerals from one to five on each numbered square (later, from one to ten in each square). Begin as a matching exercise first and then go to rote memory.
    h. Have the student count different groupings of children in the class.
    i. The student can count pennies, boxes, cylinders, and stars in the flag, etc.
    j. The student can count things by categories in the classroom such as the number of pieces of chalk, erasers, books on a shelf, etc.

CHAP. 6   Task Level Curriculum

7. AUDITORY–VISUAL SYMBOL ASSOCIATION

   a. Begin with wooden, plastic, felt, or magnetic numerals and have the student arrange them in order from one to five and later from one to ten. The teacher says a numeral, holds it up, and the child matches by pointing to the correct one.
   b. The student can copy from a model as the teacher says each numeral.
   c. The student can look in newspapers or magazines for numerals which he later can identify for the teacher.
   d. Use ditto sheets where the child circles all of one number while he says the number.
   e. Use color by number games. The teacher says a number and he colors the area containing the number. The completed area colored by the child should form an identifiable design.

8. SYMBOL–VALUE ASSOCIATION (SETS)

   a. Use "Pop It Beads" and say "Show me one," etc.
      1) ●
      2) ● ●
      3) ● ● ●
   b. Use the Maria Montessori formula as follows:
      1. Say, "This is (●) one."
         "This is (● ●) two."
         "This is (● ● ●) three."
      2) Put them in order.
      3) Say, "Show me one."   ●
         "Show me two."   ● ●
         "Show me three."   ● ● ●
      4) Say, "Give me one."   ●
         "Give me two."   ● ●
         "Give me three."   ● ● ●
      Make another set the same size as Item 1 above and label as follows:
      Say, "This is [●]."
         "This is [● ●]."
         "This is [● ● ●]."
   c. Use a pegboard and have the student say the correct numeral as he matches the number of pegs with the symbol equivalent. For example,
   d. Use beads, buttons, blocks, or coins to correspond with numerals from one to five (later from one to ten).
   e. The student can name things that come in two's such as feet, eyes, ears, hands, etc.; in three's such as tricycle wheels, or a three legged stool, etc.; in fours such as dog's legs, chair legs, table legs, car's tires, etc.; in five's such as fingers, toes, pennies to a nickel, points on a star, etc.

Arithmetic

    f. The student can make impressions of groups in clay using pennies, beans, dowels, etc.

    g. The student can find pictures in magazines or books of different numbers of items.

    h. Playing cards are good for learning and identifying sets.

    i. Small cans labeled from one to ten with corresponding ice-cream sticks or counters in them can be used to teach symbol–value associations (sets).

8. CARDINAL AND ORDINAL RELATIONSHIPS

    a. Begin with three or four toy cars in a line near a toy house or a garage and ask the following questions:
       1) Which one is closest?
       2) Which one is farthest away?
       3) Which car is at the beginning of the line?
       4) Which car is at the end of the line?
          Note: As the child responds, the teacher should say, "Yes, this is the first car, or second car," etc., as necessary.
       5) Continue to ask questions about the third car, fourth car, etc.

    b. Give the student number cards and teach the cardinal values of one to five first and later to ten. Have the students line up in groups of five or ten, and as a teacher calls the cardinal number, the child with that number holds it up.

    c. Play "office building" and decide on what floors certain things will need to go.

    d. Label your book shelves, first, second, third, fourth, etc.

    e. After the children can read the words, begin using cardinal directions when putting assignments on the chalkboard.

    f. Use in everyday activities in the classroom such as when lining up the class, say, "Row one will line up first, row five will line up second, etc."

9. SIMPLE ADDITION AND SUBTRACTION

    a. Alignment can be taught with "see through" color pens:

    b. Use concrete materials at first where objects such as rods can represent one or entire groupings. For example,

    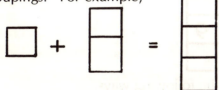

    c. Basic addition and subtraction number facts can be written on small oaktag strips and placed in small "draw string" cloth bags. The student can reach into the bags and pull them out. The answers can be written on the back of the cards to make them self-checking.

147

CHAP. 6   Task Level Curriculum

d. Addition and subtraction facts should be taught using ditto sheets in all of the following ways:

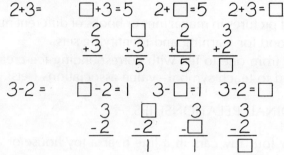

10. SIMPLE MULTIPLICATION

   a. Begin by teaching "skip counting," for example, 2, 4, 6, 8, 10, 12, 14, 16, 18, 20, 22, 24. (1) The student can begin with "pop it" beads or blocks and also simultaneously work on small ditto sheets where the teacher has written the first and ending numeral, for example,

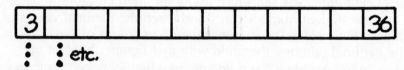

   The student can count the beads and write the numerals in that way checking his work. (2) After the student has learned to skip count from two through ten, he can do larger ditto sheets with many different numeral combinations. The teacher can make up ditto sheets with blanks so they can be used for any numeral.

   b. When the student has learned all of his skip counting, he can begin to use matrix sheets. The student can put the numerals across the top and down the left hand side using different colored pencils. He can then fill in the matrix working down or across. This will help him to see that 4 × 3 for example, is the same as 3 × 4.

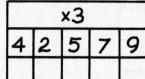

   c. By using ditto sheets with numerals on them, the teacher can fill in the multiplication fact he wants the student to practice by putting it on top of the page. For example,

×3				
4	2	5	7	9

   d. Teach multiplication in all of the following ways:

   3×4=   □×4=12   3×□=12   3×4=□

   ```
     4      4      □      4
   ×3    ×□    ×3    ×3
   ───   ───   ───   ───
    12    12    12     □
   ```

148

Arithmetic

e. The student can also do "arrays" whereby the student counts the intersections.

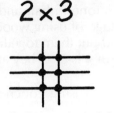

f. Multiplication drills are helpful.

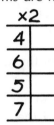
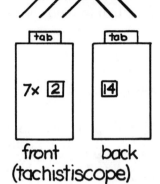

front / back
(tachistiscope)

11. SIMPLE DIVISION

a. Teach initially using "pop it" beads or blocks which the student groups according to the teacher's directions. For example, "How many groups of 3 equal 6."

b. Distributing buttons or coins equally or with a remainder to fellow students is a good activity.

c. A numberline can be used to teach simple division with remainder. For example,

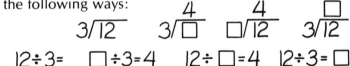

d. Simple matrix sheets can also be used to teach division. For example,

÷	10	8	6	4	2
2	5	4			

e. Teach division in all of the following ways:

$3\overline{)12}$ $3\overline{)\square}$ $\square\overline{)12}$ $3\overline{)12}$

$12 \div 3 =$ $\square \div 3 = 4$ $12 \div \square = 4$ $12 \div 3 = \square$

f. Simple drills to include the following are helpful:

```
÷4
 8
16
36
24
```

12. SIMPLE FRACTIONS

a. Teach division of shapes and sets by using concrete objects then repeat these on the ditto sheets. For example,

149

CHAP. 6   Task Level Curriculum

    b. Make a set of materials out of wooden dowels. Take a rod of 24-inch long dowling and cut it into six 4 inch pieces. Leave four of the pieces whole to use for teaching division of sets and cut the other two pieces (one in half and one in fourths) to use in teaching division of shapes. The advantage of using wooden dowling is that the child can hold 2 or 4 pieces in his hands and put them together to see the whole, or he can line the 4 dowels up and see that ½ of 4 is 2. They are also good for tracing around prior to working the problem.

    c. After the student understands simple fractions using concrete objects, the teacher can then introduce him to ditto sheets.

13. CONSERVATION OF QUANTITY

    a. Pour equal amounts of sand into two containers of the same size ([image]) then pour one container of sand into another long, thin container ([image]); finally pour the contents of the 2nd container into a short, wide container ([image]). Ask the student to tell you which one has more sand. If he does not understand, reverse the process; and then repeat it.

    b. Use money to teach conservation of quantity beginning with a nickel equals five pennies, two nickels equal a dime, or a nickel and five pennies equal a dime, etc.

    c. Use rods or dowels to represent different sizes. There is also a great deal of commercial material available to teach this concept.

    d. Count out twenty sticks with a student. Make four bundles of five sticks each. Take two bundles of five sticks and make one bundle of ten sticks. Tell the student that one bundle of ten sticks equals two bundles of five sticks. The student should check by counting. The student can then be told that one bundle of ten sticks and two bundles of five sticks equal the twenty sticks he started out with. He should count to check.

    e. Fill a small measuring spoon full of water. Suck up the water with an eye dropper. Count the drops as they are squeezed back into the spoon. Did the amount stay the same when it was put back in the spoon drop by drop?

14. PROCESS SIGNS

    a. Begin by using wooden, plastic, sandpaper, or magnetic numerals including process signs.

    b. Blocks with numerals and process signs can also be used.

    c. Use ditto sheets which include the following forms:

$$\Box + \Box = \quad \Box - \Box = \quad \Box \times \Box = \quad \Box \div \Box =$$

$$\begin{array}{c}\Box\\+\Box\end{array} \quad \begin{array}{c}\Box\\-\Box\end{array} \quad \begin{array}{c}\Box\\\times\Box\end{array}$$

    d. Teach greater than and less than using beads, blocks, or rods.
Two is greater than one: ⁚>•. One is less than two: •<⁚
The greater amount fits into the largest opening.

    e. Use color coded draw string bags marked with the appropriate process sign that

Arithmetic

contain arithmetic problems on small oaktag strips. For example, a pink bag will contain pink strips of oaktag with addition problems.

15. MEASUREMENT

    a. Begin by rechecking the estimation ability of the student.
    b. Use a yardstick and have the student measure the perimeter of the room.
    c. Pour two pints of liquid into a quart jar and then four quarts into a gallon container.
    d. Color each foot in a yardstick a different color.
    e. The student can measure his desk and other areas of the room with a ruler.
    f. Use ditto sheets and rulers (first to include inches and later to half inches) and have the student measure lines of different length.
    g. The student should draw his own lines and tell you how long they are.
    h. Obtain a scale so the student can determine the relative weights of objects in the classroom.
    i. The student should use a scale in order to better understand the concepts of equivalency. For example, sixteen ounces equal a pound.

16. MAPS AND GRAPHS

    a. Three dimensional or raised forms can be used to teach maps and graphs.
    b. Clay can be used to teach land forms such as peninsular, isthmus, island, lake, etc.
    c. Develop a globe using a balloon covered with paper mache and then painted.
    d. Draw simple maps of the classroom and have the child pace off and draw it to scale.
    e. The student can draw a map of his bedroom and then of his house.
    f. Older students enjoy designing their own treasure maps. This is an effective method of teaching the concepts of land forms, map legends, etc.
    g. Graphs can be constructed from strips of oaktag and colored construction paper.
    h. The student can graph his own progress in arithmetic and other subject areas.
    i. The student can graph baseball and football scores as well as scores in other sports and games.

GLOSSARY

Abstract Level. A higher level of conceptualization or thinking that involves the ability to see relationships based on difference and sameness as it pertains to classification and association in all of life's experiences. An abstract response would be that an apple and an orange are both fruit.

Acuity. A sensory level function that pertains to keenness of sight, hearing, or touch. Acuity is a primary level function in terms of input where learning is concerned.

Amount of Input. The quantity of information that is presented to the learner in a given period of time through any or all of the learning channels.

Analysis. The decoding of information. Along with synthesis it forms the essentials of an integrative system resulting in the formulation of concepts and in the constant evaluation and reevaluation of information.

Analytical approach. In reading, the learner would begin with a configuration or the whole word first and then break it down into its components or sound segments.

Aphasia. A disorder of language or symbolization resulting from neurological impairment that manifests itself in disorders of reception (comprehension of the spoken word) or expression where the individual loses from partially to completely his ability to speak even though he knows what he wants to say.

Articulation. The execution of speech. Disorders of speech are manifested in the form of omissions (leaving out sounds), substitutions (*teef* for *teeth*), distortions (lisping), or additions (*skippering* for *skipping*).

Associative learning. The process of reinforcing learning by relating concepts or new learning to visual, auditory, or tactual associations to the extent that it will enable the learner to stabilize (retain) that which has been taught. For example, a word is written on a card; and an associative picture clue is put on the back of the same card.

Attention. The ability to focus (attend) auditorily and/or visually to stimuli or input for a period of time without losing the context or content of that which is being presented.

Auditory to auditory association. The ability to relate a sound to a sound (phonemes). The student can relate the sound of "t" in *time* to the sound of "t" in *touch* and transfer the association to different situations. When presented with three toys, all of which begin with different sounds, the learner will identify the toy which begins with a specific sound as indicated by the instructor.

Glossary

Auditory channel. The processing of information that is essentially auditory in nature at different levels to include sensory (hearing), perception (localization, attention, discrimination, closure, figure-ground), imagery (memory-sequencing), and auditory language functions (classification and association).

Auditory language association. The ability to understand auditorily non-categorical relationships between words or experiences presented orally. The individual can discern that a "boat" goes with "water" rather than with "sky."

Auditory language classification. The ability to understand categorical relationships between words or experiences presented orally. The individual can discern that "apple" goes with "peach" rather than with "chair."

Auditory to visual associations. The ability to relate a sound to a symbol. The student can associate the sound of "m" or its letter name to the written symbol *m* and tranfer this association to different situations, such as an *m* in words printed on the chalkboard, or on a paper at his desk, etc.

Aural. Processes that are essentially auditory in nature.

Balance and coordination. The ability to use both sides of the body simultaneously, individually, or alternately.

Basal reader. A developmentally organized system of reading that is based upon a sight-word vocabulary emphasizing a "look, say" approach.

Binocular fusion. The process of integrating the overlapping portions of the visual fields into a single set of visual information.

Body image. The inner awareness of self in terms of where the parts of the body are located and their relationship to each other and to the environment.

Body rhythm. The inner awareness of rhythm in terms of body movement as may be observed in walking, running, marching, and keeping time to music.

Central blindness (object recognition). The inability to integrate visual stimuli into a uniform whole, or the inability to recognize objects. The individual tends to focus his attention on the parts.

Cerebral dominance. The establishment of one hemisphere of the brain as dominant over the other hemisphere. This is generally considered prerequisite for the establishment of the preferred use of the left or right hand in children.

Closure. The ability to formulate auditorily or visually a whole word from its component parts. In reading, this is called blending.

Compensatory processing. The utilization of intact learning processes or open channels to compensate for other learning processes or correlates which are deficient. If the learner cannot remember what he hears, he can use visual or tactual associative clues to help him remember or retain that which has been taught.

Conceptualization. The cognitive processing of information or experiences (thinking) at three basic levels:

1. *Concrete level:*
   A peach is round and has a fuzzy skin.
2. *Functional level:*
   The peach can be eaten or made into preserves.

Glossary

3. *Abstract level:*
   A peach is a fruit.

Concrete level. Thinking, conceptualization, or ideation that primarily deals with experiences at a descriptive level. For example, a pencil is made out of wood; it has lead and an eraser. The concrete level of presentation on the other hand indicates the utilization of concrete objects in introducing concepts to learners.

Control factors. Factors that affect the control of learner behavior within the learning environment, a few of which are distractibility, disinhibition, and perseveration.

Convergence. The coordinated movements of the eyes that are necessary for focusing an image on the fovea.

Critical skills. Process-oriented skills that are critical for the acquisition of academic tasks, such as reading, writing, spelling and arithmetic. For example, auditory discrimination is a prerequisite critical skill for learning phonics.

Cueing. A teaching technique used in aiding learners with expressive language disorders to retrieve the correct word, i. e., "I kick with my _____?"

Decoding. The ability to assign meaning to experiences that include verbal behavior (speech, reading, and writing) as well as non-verbal behavior (gestures, expressions, and body movements).

Deficit level. Abilities or processes, which can be called learning disabilities when deficient in specific cognitive areas as they relate to learning. These deficient processes keep the learner from succeeding at the task level skills of reading, writing, spelling, and arithmetic. A deficit in auditory discrimination may cause problems with phonics.

Developmental inventories. Reading, writing, spelling, and arithmetic inventories that measure these skills in a developmental manner, giving the independent, instructional, and frustration levels of functioning.

Directionality. The relationship of an object or point in space to another object or point in space. Difficulty in this developmental skill may result in left–right confusion in reading and writing.

Discrimination. A process under the category of perception that denotes the ability of the learner to discern likenesses and differences between sounds and between symbols.

Disinhibition. Inability to control verbal behavior as exemplified by the learner who gets carried away by his own thoughts and offers unrelated responses to that which is being discussed.

Distractibility. Exhibiting "forced attention" to extraneous stimuli resulting in poor overall attention and reduced on-task behavior.

Encoding. The aspect of communication that involves output through the act of motor language expression (manual, body movement, and speech), verbal language expression (retrieval, syntax, and formulation), and written expressive language.

Expressive language. The ability to communicate by using words verbally, by writing, or by using gestures that describe or indicate a quality, a function, or a relationship.

Eye–Foot coordination. The learner controls movements of the feet through the coordination of the eye, foot, and brain which operate in concert with each other at the automatic level of functioning.

Faulty learning responses. The stabilization in the learner of faulty learning habits or responses established in order to meet the demands of parents, teachers, and peers to achieve specific tasks. The student may develop an unorthodox pencil grip due to early inappropriate pressure and frustration with beginning writing.

Glossary

Figurative language. One of the integrative functions of auditory language association. Learners with problems in this area have difficulty understanding such phrases as "He blew up," meaning he was angry.

Figure–Ground. A sub-category of perception that involves the ability to separate at will what one wishes to attend to visually or auditorily (figure) from the surrounding environment (ground).

Fine motor (eye–hand coordination). The purposeful coordinated movements of the hand and eye operating in concert with thought patterns to achieve a specific motor task such as writing, sorting, and sewing.

Formulation. The smooth and natural flow of language in terms of organizing thought processes into concise patterns for verbal expression and for writing.

Frustration level. In reading, this would be the level at which the learner exhibits tension, hesitations, word-by-word reading, and low comprehension. Oral reading is below 93%, and comprehension is below 75%.

Grapheme. The visual representation for a symbol which includes letters, words, and numerals.

Gross motor. Movement that involves balance, coordination, and large muscle activity, as required for efficiency in walking, running, skipping, jumping, and other physical activities.

Gustatory. Related to the sense of taste.

Handedness. The consistent use of one hand over the other.

Haptic processing. The processing of cutaneous or tactual (touch) and kinesthetic (body movement) information.

Hyperactivity. An unusual amount of movement for a learner considering his age and the physical setting in which the excessive movement is taking place.

Imagery. Overall memory including the ability to remember or retain both in sequence and out of sequence that which has been seen, heard, or felt for both long and short periods of time.

Independent level. The level at which a student will work at ease without having to be under the constant direction of the instructor. In reading, for example, the learner will make less than four errors in one hundred consecutive words with 90% or better in comprehension.

Inhibiting responses. Holding back or controlling motor expression or behavior due mainly to pressure from parents, teachers, or peers. The learner may expend a great deal of energy, suffer anxiety, and even withdraw if he does not have opportunities to "act out" or "respond motorically" within a structured environment.

Inner-language. The language of thinking utilized for the integration of experiences. A native language which can be labeled inner-speech.

Input. Any information coming in through the auditory, visual, tactual, kinesthetic, olfactory, or gustatory modalities, the rate, amount, and sequence of which often determines success or failure in school.

Instructional level. The point at which the teacher's aid is necessary. Following instruction, however, the learner should be able to continue with the material independently. In reading, he should be able to read with at least 93% accuracy in word recognition and with 76% or better in comprehension.

Jamming. Giving the learner too much input too rapidly. One more spelling word or sound may result in forgetting. The learner may fail at the task if he is required to "hold" too much information at a given time.

Glossary

Kinesthetic. The awareness of and adjustment to one's environment in terms of body movement. The potential for using body movement has not been fully explored in teaching children.

Language. The ability to apply meaning to words and other symbols based on one's experiences and to express oneself through a motor act or through clear sequential verbal thought patterns.

Laterality. The establishment of sidedness and the concomitant ability to relate oneself physically to an object in space.

Linguistic approach to reading. A whole-word approach that builds vocabulary on the basis of spelling patterns rather than nonsense syllables. For example, using a consonant–vowel–consonant pattern, the consonant "c" combined with the spelling pattern "at" gives cat. The consonants "b," "p," "m," etc. added to the same pattern will give other words.

Listening comprehension. The highest level at which the learner can understand 75% of the material read to him.

Localization (auditory). Locating the source and direction of sound. The learner may have difficulty in discerning that different people have different voices or that a particular voice is specific to one particular person.

Manipulatives. A material that involves the learner in a motor act such as building symbols out of clay, or in wet sand, or working with blocks or beads, etc.

Manual expression. To be able to express the function or quality of an object through showing by using the hands and other parts of the body in meaningful gestures.

Maturational lag. Slower development in some of the critical areas of learning. This includes deficits in the physical, social-emotional, and cognitive processes in the learner who has near average, average, or above average intellectual functioning that will hamper him (if not developed) in the acquisition of academic skills.

Modality. Avenues of input to include auditory, visual, tactual–kinesthetic, olfactory, and gustatory approaches.

Motor. That which requires movement or muscular activity.

Multi-sensory approach. The utilization of many modalities or avenues of input simultaneously in teaching. The student will see, hear, and touch at the same time when presented a particular task.

Non-verbal language. The ability to assign meaning to gestures and expressions (body language) as well as to such cultural phenomena as art, music, holidays, or patriotism.

Ocular motor. Eye movements in visually examining the individual details of an object to include distinguishing light from no light, seeing fine detail, binocular fusion, convergence, and scanning.

Olfactory. Related to the sense of smell.

On-task behavior. Learner activity that is directed specifically toward the task as specified by the teacher and not extraneous to the task. For example, when the student is assigned the task of reading he is doing more than just holding the book.

Open channel. The channel(s) including auditory, visual, or tactual–kinesthetic that provide the learner with accurate information, in that they are intact and not deficient. This includes the various processing levels of sensation, perception, imagery, and language. Helen Keller learned essentially through the tactual–kinesthetic approach (her open channel).

Output. The processes involved in encoding that include motor responses (manual and body movement) as well as verbal responses (speech, syntax, and formulation).

Glossary

Overstimulation. Too much input for the learner to cope with which may result in excessive motor activity, anxiety, poor attention, reduced learning, or any combination of these.

Perception. A lower level of learning which can be described as more brain function in that it encompasses the sub-areas of discrimination, figure–ground, closure, and localization and attention as pertains to the visual and auditory processing of information.

Perseveration. The inability to use "stop and go" mechanisms efficiently; the learner will tend to repeat an act when it is no longer appropriate. He may have difficulty in shifting from one activity to another. For example, on tests he may repeat the previous response.

Phoneme. The sound that is assigned to a symbol that may be used in different ways, i.e., the "p" in *pen* and the "p" in *spoon* are one phoneme.

Plateau. The level beyond which point the learner makes no significant progress in academic tasks.

Rate of input. How fast information is presented to the learner in a given period of time.

Readability. A formula which can be applied to written material to obtain a grade placement.

Re-auditorization. The ability to retrieve auditory images.

Receptive language. The ability to apply meaning to words based on experiences in terms of classification and association contingencies.

Retrieval. The ability to recall words for use in speaking and writing.

Revisualization. The ability to recall visual images or to see the image in the "mind's eye."

Scanning. To perform the natural zig-zag movements of the eyes when shifting from image to image. This has also been referred to as "visual tracking," "visual pursuit," or the systematic learned eye movements required for reading.

Sensation. The lowest level of learning at which the learner receives initial input through his auditory (hearing), visual (seeing), tactual–kinesthetic (feeling), olfactory (smelling), or gustatory (taste) senses.

Sequence of input. The order of input (visual–auditory–tactual) or presentation of information and material.

Sequencing. The ability to remember in order that which has been heard, seen, or felt for both long and short periods of time.

Social perception. The ability to glean meaning from gestures and expressions or from what may appear to be easily discernible cause–effect relationships.

Spacing. The introduction of new material or concepts far enough apart to avoid confusion on the part of the learner:
  t and *d* spaced (aural)
  t and *f* spaced (visual)
  p and *b* spaced (aural and visual).

Spatial orientation. The ability to organize space in terms of the individual relating his physical self to the environment with reference to distance, size, position, and direction.

Suppression. The individual suppresses the image coming in from a less effective eye in order to avoid a double image resulting in the less effective eye becoming non-functional.

Syntax. The ability to structure thoughts into grammatically correct verbal units or sentences.

Symbolization. A synonym for language in that a symbol represents something in a way that provides the interpreter or learner with meaning at both verbal and non-verbal levels.

Glossary

Synthetic approach. In reading this would be a part-to-whole approach beginning with letter sounds and then blending the sounds into words.

Tachistoscope. A device with which the instructor can control the presentation of visual material (words) with precise time exposures.

Tactual. Related to the sense of touch.

Telegraphic speech. A deficit in verbal language expression under the sub-area of syntax and formulation whereby the learner speaks like a telegram reads, i.e. hungry—give money—go eat.

Temporal orientation. The ability to order and organize time efficiently.

Transition writing approach. A bridging technique that transitions learners from manuscript to cursive writing by using connecting dots and tracing.

Understimulated. Not enough input resulting in a poor learning environment where learners exhibit little motivation or interest.

Verbal language expression. A sub-area under receptive language that includes word retrieval, syntax, and formulation.

Visual channel. All of the processes that are involved in the visual aspects of learning to include sensation, perception, imagery, and language, as well as the related areas of visual motor integration.

Visual language association. The cognitive ability to understand non-categorical relationships between pictures of objects or experiences presented visually. The individual can discern that a picture of a pen goes with a picture of a pencil rather than with a picture of a bucket.

Visual language classification. The cognitive ability to understand categorical relationships between objects or experiences presented visually. The individual can discern that a picture of an airplane goes with a picture of a car rather than with a picture of a tree.

Visual-motor. The ability to synchronize or coordinate the eyes with the movements of the hand and the thought processes of the brain. Efficiency of these three processes operating in concert with each other is required for handwriting and other motor tasks.

Word caller. A learner who has mastered the mechanics of reading words but who cannot apply meaning to these words based on his experiences.

Glossary

BIBLIOGRAPHY

Adams, G. *Measurement in Education, Psychology, and Guidance.* New York: Holt, Rinehart, and Winston, Inc., 1964.

Ahr, E. *Screening Test of Academic Readiness.* Skokie, Ill.: Priority Innovations, Inc., 1966.

Allen, R., and Allen, C. *Language Experiences in Reading.* Chicago: Encyclopedia Britannica Press, 1966.

Anderson, P. *Language Skills in Elementary Education.* New York: The Macmillan Company, 1964.

Ayres Southern California Figure–Ground Visual Perception Test. Los Angeles: Western Psychological Services, 1969.

Baker, H., and Leland, B. *Detroit Tests of Learning Aptitude.* Indianapolis: Test Division of Bobbs-Merrill Company, 1959.

Bangs, T. *Language and Learning Disorders of the Pre-Academic Child.* New York: Appleton-Century-Crofts, 1968.

Barrett, T. "Visual Discrimination Tasks as Predictors of First Grade Reading Achievement." *Reading Teacher* 18 (1965), 276–282.

Barsch, R. *Enriching Perception and Cognition,* vol. 2. Seattle, Wash.: Special Child Publications, 1968.

Barsch, R. *Achieving Perceptual Motor Efficiency.* Seattle, Wash.: Special Child Publications, 1967.

Beery, K. *Developmental Test of Visual Motor Integration: Administration and Scoring Manual.* Chicago: Follett Educational Corp., 1967.

Bellak, L. and Bellak, S. *Children's Apperception Test.* New York: C.P.S. Company, 1949–1955.

Bellak, L. *Thematic Apperception Test.* New York: C.P.S. Company, 1954.

Bender, L. *A Visual Motor Gestalt Test and Its Clinical Use.* New York: American Orthopsychiatric Association, 1938.

Bibliography

Benton, A. *The Revised Visual Retention Test: Clinical and Experimental Application*. New York: The Psychological Corp., 1963.

Benyon, S. *Intensive Programming for Slow Learners*. Columbus, Ohio: Charles E. Merrill Co., 1968.

Bereiter, C., and Englemann, S. *Teaching Disadvantaged Children in The Preschool*. Englewood Cliffs, N.J.: Prentice-Hall, 1966.

Bernstein, B. *Everyday Problems and the Child with Learning Difficulties*. New York: John Day Co., 1969.

Bieliauskas, V. *The House-Tree-Person H-T-P Research Review*. Los Angeles: Western Psychological Services, 1963.

Birch, H., and Gussow, J. *Disadvantaged Children: Health, Nutrition and School Failure*. New York: Grune & Stratton, Inc., 1970.

Birch, H., and Belmost, L. "Auditory-Visual Integration in Brain-Damaged and Normal Children." *Developmental Medicine and Child Neurology* 20 (1965) 135–144.

Birch, H., ed. *Brain Damage in Children: The Biological and Social Aspects*. Baltimore: Williams and Wilkins, 1964.

Boehm Test of Basic Concepts. New York: The Psychological Corp., 1970.

Bond, G., and Tinker, M. *Reading Difficulties: Their Diagnosis and Correction*. 2nd ed. New York: Appleton-Century-Crofts, 1967.

Boston University Speech Sound Discrimination Picture Test. Boston: Boston University School of Education, 1955.

Brenner, A. *The Anton Brenner Developmental Gestalt Test of School Readiness*. Los Angeles: Western Psychological Services, 1964.

Bruner, J. *The Process of Education*. New York: Vintage Books, 1963.

Bryngelson, B., and Glaspey, E. *Speech in the Classroom*. 3d ed. Chicago: Scott, Foresman Co., 1962.

Cardboard Snellen Charts for School Use. Chicago: American Medical Association.

Chall, J. *Learning to Read: The Great Debate*. New York: McGraw-Hill Book Co., 1967.

Chaney, C., and Kephart, N. *Motoric Aids to Perceptual Training*. Columbus, Ohio: The Charles E. Merrill Co., 1968.

Cheves, R. *Visual–Motor Perception Teaching Materials*, Boston: Teaching Resources Corp., 1967.

Clymer, T., and Barrett, T. *Clymer-Barrett Pre-Reading Battery*. Princeton, N.J.: Personnel Press, Inc., 1969.

Clymer, T., Christenson, B., and Russell, D. *Building Pre-Reading Skills: Kit A, Language*. Boston: Ginn and Company, 1965.

Combs, A., ed. *Perceiving, Behaving, Becoming: A New Focus for Education*. Washington, D. C.: Association for Supervision and Curriculum Development, 1962.

Cratty, B. *Active Learning: Games to Enhance Academic Abilities*. Englewood Cliffs, N.J.: Prentice-Hall, Inc., 1971.

Cratty, B. *Perceptual–Motor Behavior and Educational Processes*. Springfield, Ill.: Charles C. Thomas, 1969.

Cratty, B. *Developmental Sequences of Perceptual Motor Tasks*. New York: Educational Activities, Inc., 1967.

Cratty, B. *Movement Behavior and Motor Learning*. Philadelphia: Lea and Febiger, 1967.

Cruickshank, W. *Brain-Injured Child in Home, School, and Community*. Syracuse: Syracuse University Press, 1967.

Bibliography

Cruickshank, W., ed. *The Teacher of Brain-Injured Children.* Syracuse: Syracuse University Press, 1966.

Cruickshank, W., Bentzen, F., Ratzeburg, F., and Tannhauser, M. *A Teaching Method for Brain-Injured and Hyperactive Children.* Syracuse: Syracuse University Press, 1961.

Dale, E. and Chall, J. *A Formula for Predicting Readability.* Columbus, Ohio: Bureau of Educational Research, Ohio State University, 1948.

Daley, W. *Speech and Language Therapy with the Brain Damaged Child.* Washington, D.C.: Catholic University of America Press, 1961.

Dechant, E. *Diagnosis and Remediation of Reading Disability.* West Nyack, N.Y.: Parker Publishing Co., 1968.

deHirsch, K., Jansky, J., and Langford, W. *Predicting Reading Failure: A Preliminary Study of Reading, Writing and Spelling Disabilities in Preschool Children.* New York: Harper & Row, 1966.

Delacato, C. *The Diagnosis and Treatment of Speech and Reading Problems.* Springfield, Ill.: Charles C Thomas, 1963.

Drake, C. *P. E. R. C. Auditory Discrimination Test.* Sherborn, Mass.: Perceptual Education and Research Center, 1965.

Dunn, L., ed. *Exceptional Children in the Schools: Special Education in Transition.* 2d ed. New York: Holt, Rinehart, & Winston, Inc., 1963.

Dunn, L. *Peabody Picture Vocabulary Test.* Minneapolis: American Guidance Service, 1959.

Durrell, D. *Improving Reading Instruction,* pp. 200–201. Yonkers-on-Hudson, N.Y.: World Book Co., 1956.

Ebersole, M., Kephart, N., and Ebersole, J. *Steps to Achievement for the Slow Learner.* Columbus, Ohio: Charles E. Merrill Co., 1968.

Edgington, R. and Clements, S. *Indexed Bibliography on the Educational Management of Children with Learning Disabilities (Minimal Brain Dysfunction).* Chicago: Argus Communications, 1967.

Egg, M. *Educating the Child Who is Different.* New York: John Day Co., 1968.

Fernald, G. *Remedial Techniques in Basic School Subjects.* New York: McGraw-Hill Book Co., 1943.

Fine, B. *Underachievers.* New York: E.P. Dutton & Co., Inc., 1967.

Flesch, R. *How to Test Readability.* New York: Harper & Row, 1951.

Freeman, F. *Guiding Growth in Handwriting, Evaluation Scale.* Columbus, Ohio: Parker Zaner Bloser Co., 1958.

Friedus, E. "The Needs of Teachers for Specialized Information on Number Concepts." *The Teacher of Brain-Injured Children,* Edited by W. Cruickshank. Syracuse: Syracuse University Press, 1966.

Frierson, E., and Barbe, W., ed. *Educating Children with Learning Disabilities.* New York: Appleton-Century-Crofts, 1967.

Fries, C. *Linguistics and Reading.* New York: Holt, Rinehart and Winston, Inc., 1963.

Frostig, M., and Horne, D. "Marianne Frostig Center of Education Therapy." *Special Education Programs Within the United States,* Edited by M. Jones. Springfield, Ill.: Charles C Thomas, 1968.

Frostig, M.: *Frostig Developmental Test of Visual Perception.* Palo Alto, Calif.: Consulting Psychologists Press, Inc., 1963.

Fuller, G., and Laird, G. "Minnesota Percepto-Diagnostic Test." *Journal of Clinical Psychology* 19 (January 1963), 3–34.

Bibliography

Gates, A. *Gates Reading Readiness Scales.* New York: Bureau of Publications, Teacher's College, Columbia University, 1958.

Gearheart, B. *Learning Disabilities: Educational Strategies.* St. Louis: The C.V. Mosby Co., 1973.

Getman, G., Kane, E., Halgren, M., and McKee, G. *Developing Learning Readiness: Teachers Manual.* St. Louis: Webster Division, McGraw-Hill Book Co., 1968.

Getman, G. *How to Develop Your Child's Intelligence.* Luverne, Minn.: G.N. Getman, O.D., 1962.

Gillingham, A., and Stillman, B. *Remedial Training for Children with Specific Disability in Reading, Spelling and Penmanship.* 7th ed. Cambridge, Mass.: Educators Publishing Service, Inc., 1965.

Gitter, L. *The Montessori Way.* Seattle, Wash.: Special Child Publications, 1970.

Golden, N., and Steiner, S. "Auditory and Visual Functions in Good and Poor Readers." *Journal of Learning Disabilities* 2 (1969), 476–481.

Goldman, R., Fristoe, M. and Woodcock, R. *Goldman-Fristoe-Woodcock Test of Auditory Discrimination.* Circle Pines, Minn.: American Guidance Service, Inc., 1970.

Goodenough, F. *Draw-A-Person Test: The Measurement of Intelligence by Drawings.* Yonkers-on-Hudson, N.Y.: World Book Co., 1926.

Graham, F., and Kendall, B. *Memory-for-Designs Test.* Missoula, Mont.: Psychological Test Specialists, 1960.

Guilford, J. *The Nature of Human Intelligence.* New York: McGraw-Hill Book Co., 1967.

Hainsworth, P., and Siqueland, M. *The Meeting Street School Screening Test.* Providence, R.I.: Crippled Children and Adults of Rhode Island, Inc., 1969.

Hallahan, D., and Cruickshank, W. *Psychoeducational Foundations of Learning Disabilities.* Englewood Cliffs, N.J.: Prentice-Hall, Inc. 1973.

Hammill, D., and Bartel, N., ed. *Educational Perspectives in Learning Disabilities.* New York: John Wiley & Sons, Inc., 1971.

Haring. N., and Phillips, E. *Analysis and Modification of Classroom Behavior.* Englewood Cliffs, N.J.: Prentice-Hall, Inc., 1972.

Haring, N., and Schiefelbusch, R., ed. *Methods in Special Education.* New York: McGraw-Hill Book Co., 1967.

Haring, N., and Whelan, R., ed. *The Learning Environment: Relationship to Behavior Modification and Implications for Special Education.* Lawrence, Kan.: University of Kansas Press, 1966.

Harris, A. *Harris Test of Lateral Dominance.* 3d rev. ed. New York: Psychological Corp., 1958.

Harris, O. *Goodenough-Harris Drawing Tests.* New York: Harcourt Brace Jovanovich, 1963.

Hatton, D., Pizzat, F., and Pelkowski, J. *Perceptual-Motor Teaching Materials, Erie Program 1.* Boston: Teaching Resources, 1967.

Hebb, D. "A Neuropsychological Theory." *Psychology: A Study of a Science,* Edited by S. Kock. New York: McGraw-Hill Book Co., 1959.

Hellmuth, J., ed. *Learning Disorders, vol. 1–4.* Seattle, Wash.: Special Child Publications, 1965–1971.

Hellmuth, J., ed. *The Special Child in Century 21.* Seattle, Wash.: Special Child Publications, 1964.

Hewett, F. *The Emotionally Disturbed Child in the Classroom.* Boston: Allyn & Bacon, Inc., 1968.

Hildreth, G., Griffiths, N., and McGauvran, M. *Metropolitan Readiness Tests.* New York: Harcourt Brace Jovanovich, 1966.

Houston Test of Language Development. *The Houston Test.* Houston: Houston Press, 1963.

Ilg, F., and Ames, L. *School Readiness.* New York: Harper & Row, 1965.

Ilg, F., and Ames, L. *School Readiness.* Behavior Tests Used at the Gesell Institute. New York: Harper & Row, 1965.

Janowitz, G. *Helping Hands.* Chicago: The University of Chicago Press, 1965.

Jastak, J., Bijou, S., and Jastak, S. *Wide-Range Achievement Test.* Wilmington, Del.: Guidance Associates, 1965.

Johnson, D., and Myklebust, H. *Learning Disabilities: Educational Principles and Practices.* New York: Grune & Stratton, Inc., 1967.

Johnson, M., and Kress, R. *Informal Reading Inventories, Reading Aid Series.* Newark, Del.: International Reading Association, 1965.

Jones, V., ed. *Special Education Programs within the United States.* Springfield, Ill.: Charles C Thomas, 1968.

Karnes, M. *Helping Young Children Develop Language Skills: A Book of Activities.* Washington, D.C.: The Council for Exceptional Children, 1968.

Kass, C. "Psycholinguistic Disabilities of Children with Reading Problems." *Exceptional Children* 32 (1966), 533–539.

Kelly, T., et al. *Stanford Achievement Tests.* New York: Harcourt Brace Jovanovich, 1964.

Kephart, N. *The Slow Learner in the Classroom.* rev. ed. Columbus, Ohio: Charles E. Merrill Co., 1971.

Kephart, N. *Learning Disabilities: An Educational Adventure.* West Lafayette, Ind.: Kappa Delta Pi Press, 1968.

Kephart, N., and Roach, E. *Purdue Perceptual–Motor Survey.* Columbus, Ohio: Charles E. Merrill Co., 1966.

Keystone Visual Survey Telebinocular. Meadville, Pa.: Keystone View Co., 1958.

Kinsbourne, M., and Warrington, E. "Developmental Factors in Reading and Writing Backwardness." *The Disabled Reader: Education of the Dyslexic Child*, pp. 59–71. Edited by J. Money. Baltimore: Johns Hopkins Press, 1966.

Kirk, S., McCarthy, J., and Kirk, W. *Illinois Test of Psycholinguistic Abilities: Revised Edition, Examiners Manual.* Urbana, Ill.: University of Illinois Press, 1968.

Koppitz, E. *Children with Learning Disabilities: A Five Year Follow-Up Study.* New York: Grune & Stratton, Inc., 1971.

Koppitz, E. *The Bender Gestalt Test for Young Children.* New York: Grune & Stratton, Inc., 1964.

Landsman, M., and Dillard, H. *Evanston Early Identification Scale.* Chicago: Follett Educational Corp., 1967.

Lerner, J. *Children With Learning Disabilities.* Boston: Houghton Mifflin Co., 1971.

McDonald, E. *A Deep Test of Articulation.* Pittsburgh, Pa.: Stanwix House, Inc., 1964.

McLeod, P. *The Underdeveloped Learner.* Springfield, Ill.: Charles C Thomas Publishing Co., 1968.

Mallison, R. *Education as Therapy.* Seattle, Wash.: Special Child Publications, 1968.

Mann, P. "Dyslexia, An Educator's View," *Florida Medical Association* 56 (January 1969), 24–27.

Mann, P. "Learning Disabilities, A Critical Need for Trained Teachers." *Journal of Learning Disabilities,* vol. 2, no. 2 (February, 1969).

Bibliography

Mann, P. et. al., *Behavior Resource Guide*. Wallingford, Conn.: Educational Sciences Inc., 1973.

Massachusetts Vision Test. Boston: Massachusetts Dept. of Public Health, Welch Allyn, Inc., 1954.

Mecham, M. *Verbal Language Development Scale*. Minneapolis: American Guidance Service, 1959.

Metropolitan Achievement Tests. Tarrytown-on-Hudson, N.Y.: World Book Co., 1959.

Metropolitan Readiness Tests. New York: Harcourt Brace Jovanovich, 1950.

Michigan Picture Test and Thematic Apperception Tests. Chicago: Michigan Department of Mental Health, Science Research, 1953.

Money, J., ed. *The Disabled Reader—Education of the Dyslexic Child*. Baltimore: The Johns Hopkins Press, 1966.

Money, J., Alexander, D., and Walker, H., Jr. *A Standardized Road-Map Test of Direction Sense*. Baltimore: Johns Hopkins Press, 1965.

Montessori, M. *The Montessori Method*. Translated from the Italian by Anne E. George. Cambridge, Mass.: Robert Bentley, Inc., 1965.

Murray, H. *Thematic Apperception Test*. Cambridge, Mass.: Harvard University Press, 1943.

Myers, P., and Hammill, D. *Methods for Learning Disorders*. New York: John Wiley & Sons, Inc., 1969.

Myklebust, H., ed. *Progress in Learning Disabilities, vol. 1*. New York: Grune & Stratton, Inc., 1968.

Myklebust, H. *The Psychology of Deafness: Sensory Deprivation, Learning and Adjustment*. New York: Grune & Stratton, Inc., 1966.

Myklebust, H. *Development and Disorders of Written Language: Picture Story Language Test*. New York: Grune & Stratton, Inc., 1965.

Natchez, G., ed. *Children With Reading Problems*. New York: Basic Books, Inc., 1968.

Ortho-Rater. Rochester, N.Y.: Bausch and Lomb, Inc., 1960.

Orton, J. *A Guide to Teaching Phonics*. Cambridge, Mass.: Educators Publishing Service, 1965.

Otto, W., and McMenemy, R. *Corrective and Remedial Teaching, Principles and Practices*. Boston: Houghton Mifflin Co., 1966.

Pate, J., and Webb, W. *First Grade Screening Test*. Circle Pines, Minn.: American Guidance Service, 1966.

Perceptual Forms Test. Winter Haven, Fla.: Winter Haven Lions Club, Publications Committee, 1956.

Pronovost, W., and Dumbleton, C. "A Picture-Type Speech Sound Discrimination Test." *Journal of Speech and Hearing Disorders* 18 (1953), 258–266.

Rappaport, S., ed. *Childhood Aphasia and Brain Damage: A Definition*. Narberth, Pa.: Livingston, 1964.

Reger, R., Schroeder, W., and Uschold, K. *Special Education*. New York: Oxford University Press, 1968.

Roach, E., and Kephart, N. *The Purdue Perceptual–Motor Survey*. Columbus, Ohio: The Charles E. Merrill Co., 1966.

Roswell, F., and Chall, J. *Roswell-Chall Auditory Blending Test*. New York: The Essay Press, 1963.

Russell, R. and Kwiccinski, H. *A Program of Special Classes for Children with Learning Disabilities*. East Orange, N.J.: New Jersey Association for Brain Injured Children, 1967.

Bibliography

Siegel, E. *Helping the Brain Injured Child.* New York: Association for Brain Injured Children, 1962.

Simpson, D. *Learning to Learn.* Columbus, Ohio: Charles E. Merrill Co., 1968.

Slingerland, B. *Screening Tests for Identifying Children with Specific Language Disability.* Cambridge, Mass.: Educators Publishing Service, 1964.

Slosson, R. *Slosson Intelligence Test for Children and Adults.* East Aurora, N.Y.: Slosson Educational Publications, 1963.

Smith, R. *Teacher Diagnosis of Educational Difficulties.* Columbus, Ohio: Charles E. Merrill Co., 1969.

Spache, G. *Spache Binocular Vision Test.* Meadville, Pa.: Keystone View Co., 1961.

Spache, G. "A New Readability Formula for Primary Grade Reading Materials." *Elementary School Journal,* 53, no. 7 (March 1953), 410–413.

Special Education for Handicapped Children, First Annual Report of the National Advisory Committee on Handicapped Children. Washington, D.C.: Office of Education, Dept. of Health, Education, and Welfare, 1968.

Staats, A. *Learning, Language, and Cognition.* New York: Holt, Rinehart & Winston, Inc., 1968.

Strauss, A., and Kephart, N. *Psychopathology and Education of the Brain-Injured Child.* Progress in Theory and Clinic, vol. 2. New York: Grune & Stratton, Inc., 1955.

Strauss, A., and Lehtinen, L. *Psychopathology and Education of the Brain Injured Child.* New York: Grune & Stratton, Inc., 1947.

Stuart, M. *Neurophysiological Insights into Teaching.* Palo Alto, Calif.: Pacific Books Publishers, 1963.

Summers, E., ed. *Reading Incentive Series,* St. Louis: Webster Division, McGraw-Hill Book Co., 1968.

Templin, M., and Darley, F. *The Templin-Darley Tests of Articulation.* Iowa City: University of Iowa Bureau of Research and Service, 1960.

Terman, E., and Merrill, M. *Stanford-Binet Intelligence Scale,* Boston: Houghton Mifflin Co., 1962.

Thelan, H. *Classroom Grouping for Teachability.* New York: John Wiley & Sons, Inc., 1967.

Travers, J. *Learning Analysis and Application.* New York: Van Rees, 1965.

Valett, R. *Prescriptions for Learning.* Palo Alto, Calif.: Fearon Publishers, 1970.

Valett, R. *Programming Learning Disabilities.* Palo, Alto, Calif.: Fearon Publishers, 1969.

Valett, R. *Modifying Children's Behavior,* Palo Alto, Calif.: Fearon Publishers, 1969.

Valett, R. *A Psychoeducational Inventory of Basic Learning Abilities.* Palo Alto, Calif.: Fearon Publishers, 1968.

Valett, R. *The Remediation of Learning Disabilities.* Palo Alto, Calif.: Fearon Publishers, 1967.

Valett, R. *The Valett Developmental Survey of Basic Learning Abilities.* Palo Alto, Calif.: Consulting Psychologists Press, 1967.

Vane, J. "The Vane Kindergarten Test." *Clinical Psychology* 24 (April 1968), 1–34.

Wallace, G., and Kauffman, J. *Teaching Children with Learning Problems.* Columbus, Ohio: The Charles E. Merrill Co., 1973.

Wasserman, E., Asch, H., and Snyder, D. "A Neglected Aspect of Learning Disabilities: Energy Level Output." *Journal of Learning Disabilities* 5 (March 1972), 130–135.

Wechsler, D. *Wechsler Preschool and Primary Scale of Intelligence: Manual.* New York: The Psychological Corp., 1967.

Bibliography

Wechsler, D. *Wechsler Intelligence Scale for Children: Manual.* New York: The Psychological Corp., 1955.

Wepman, J. *Wepman Auditory Discrimination Test.* Chicago: Language Research Associates, 1958.

Wolf, M., et al. "The Timer-Game: A Variable Interval Contingency for the Management of Out-of-Seat Behavior." *Exceptional Children* 37 (October 1970), 113–118.

Young, M. *Teaching Children With Special Learning Needs.* New York: John Day Co., 1967.

Younie, W. *Instructional Approaches to Slow Learners.* New York: Teachers College Press, 1967.